Market Research Handbook

Market Research Handbook

Measurement, Approach and Practice

Jie Xu

iUniverse, Inc.
New York Lincoln Shanghai

Market Research Handbook
Measurement, Approach and Practice

Copyright © 2005 by Jie Xu

iUniverse books may be ordered through booksellers or by contacting:

iUniverse
2021 Pine Lake Road, Suite 100
Lincoln, NE 68512
www.iuniverse.com
1-800-Authors (1-800-288-4677)

ISBN-13: 978-0-595-36401-5 (pbk)
ISBN-13: 978-0-595-80836-6 (ebk)
ISBN-10: 0-595-36401-2 (pbk)
ISBN-10: 0-595-80836-0 (ebk)

Printed in the United States of America

Contents

Chapter 3

Chapter 4

Chapter 5

List of Charts

List of Figures

Chapter 1

Introduction

The measurement theory shaped up half a century ago which has been calibrated many times by theoretical practitioners and knowledge workers in various walks of science, mathematics, statistics, psychology, etc. Nowadays widely-accepted systematic measurement framework is being utilized in all measuring fields to help understand various objects.

Measurement Definition

Measurement is the determination of the size or magnitude of something. Measurement is not limited to physical quantities, but can extend to quantifying almost any imaginable thing such as degree of uncertainty, consumer confidence, or the rate of increase in the fall in the price of beanie babies. Different kinds of quantity, however, are measured at different levels of measurement.

In physics and engineering, measurement is the process of comparing physical quantities of real-world objects and events. Established standard objects and events are used as units, and the measurement results in at least two numbers for the relationship between the item under study and the referenced unit of measurement, where at least one number estimates the statistical uncertainty in the measurement, also referred to as measurement error (in a philosophical distinction). Measuring instruments are the means by which this translation is made.

For example, the unit for length might be a well-known person's foot, and the length of a boat can be given as the number of times that person's foot would fit the length of the boat.

Likewise, the measurement addressed by William Bradford Shockley, a Nobel Prize winner in physicsv (1956), "A measurement is a comparison to a standard."

When measuring an object, essentially all work is counting the number of standard pieces it takes to be the same size as the object. For example, the length of an Olympic swimming pool is 50 m, because 50 one metre standard lengths would be exactly the same length.

The same principle works when dealing with something that is too small to be conveniently handled by straight counting of standard pieces. For example, the heights of people or of trees are not usually an exact number of meters. So, simply saying that the standard meter is actually a group of smaller standard lengths—centimeters. Each centimeter can also be a group of still smaller objects—millimeters. So we can describe or measure anything simply by counting the number of standard or groups.

There is a slight problem when we consider fractal geometry, but for our purposes, counting of standard sized pieces leads to the mathematical description of size.

The contemporary complete definition of measurement turns out in psychometric theory by S. S. Stevens (1951) where measurement is determined to "consist of rules for assigning numbers to attributes of objects based upon rules". [1]

By definition any set of rules for assigning numbers to attributes of objects is measurement. Not all measurement techniques are equally useful in dealing with the world, however, and it is the function of the scientist to select those that are more useful. The physical and biological scientists generally have well-established, standardized, systems of measurement. A scientist knows, for example, what is meant when a "ghundefelder fish" is described as 10.23 centimeters long and weighing 34.23 grams. The social scientist does not, as a general rule, have such established and recognized systems. A description of an individual as having 23 "units" of need for achievement does not evoke a great deal of recognition from most scientists. For this reason the social scientist, more than the physical or biological scientist, has been concerned about the nature and meaning of measurement systems.

Properties of Measurement System

S. S. Stevens (1951) [1] described properties of measurement systems that allowed decisions about the quality or goodness of a measurement technique. A property of a measurement system deals with the extent that the relationships which exists between the attributes of objects in the "real world" are preserved in the numbers which are assigned these objects. For an example of relationships existing in the "real world", if the attribute in question is height, then objects (people) in the "real world" have more or less of the attribute (height) than other objects (people). In a similar manner, numbers have relationships to other numbers. For example 59 is less than 62, 48 equals 48, and 73 is greater than 68. One property of a measurement system that measures height, then, is whether the relationships between heights in the "real world" are preserved in the numbers which are assigned to heights; that is, whether taller individuals are given bigger numbers.

Before describing in detail the properties of measurement systems, a means of symbolizing the preceding situation—mathematical formalism is presented here.

Objects in the real world may be represented by O_i where "O" is a shorthand notation for "object" and "i" is a subscript referring to which object is being described and may take on any integer number. For example O_1 is the first object, O_2 the second, O_3 the third and so on. The symbol $M(O_i)$ will be used to symbolize the number, or measure (M), of any particular object which is assigned to that object by the system of rules; $M(O_1)$ being the number assigned to the first object, $M(O_2)$ the second, and so on. The expression $O_1 > O_2$ means that the first object has more of something in the "real world" than does the second. The expression $M(O_1) > M(O_2)$ means that the number assigned to the first object is greater than that assigned to the second.

In mathematical terms measurement is a functional mapping from the set of objects $\{O_i\}$ to the set of real numbers $\{M(O_i)\}$.

Chart 1.1 Mathematical formalism of measurement system

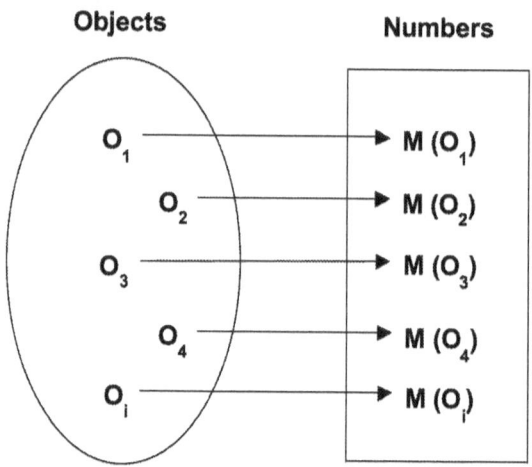

The goal of measurement systems is to structure the rule for assigning numbers to objects in such a way that the relationship between the objects is preserved in the numbers assigned to the objects. The different kinds of relationships preserved are called properties of the measurement system.

Magnitude

The property of magnitude exists when an object that has more of the attribute than another object, is given a bigger number by the rule system. This relationship must hold for all objects in the "real world". Mathematically speaking, this property may be described as follows:

The property of magnitude exists when for all i, j if $O_i > O_j$, then $M(O_i) > M(O_j)$.

Intervals

The property of intervals is concerned with the relationship of differences between objects. If a measurement system possesses the property of intervals it means that the unit of measurement means the same thing throughout the scale of numbers.

That is, an inch is an inch is an inch, no matter was it falls—immediately ahead or a mile down the road.

More precisely, an equal difference between two numbers reflects an equal difference in the "real world" between the objects that were assigned the numbers. In order to define the property of intervals in the mathematical notation, four objects are required: O_i, O_j, O_k, and O_l. The difference between objects is represented by the "-" sign; $O_i - O_j$ refers to the actual "real world" difference between object i and object j, while $M(O_i) - M(O_j)$ refers to differences between numbers.

The property of intervals exists, for all i, j, k, l if $O_i - O_j \geq O_k - O_l$ then $M(O_i) - M(O_j) \geq M(O_k) - M(O_l)$.

A corollary to the preceding definition is that if the number assigned to two pairs of objects are equally different, then the pairs of objects must be equally different in the real world. Mathematically it may be stated.

If the property of intervals exists if for all i, j, k, l if $M(O_i) - M(O_j) = M(O_k) - M(O_l)$ then $O_i - O_j = O_k - O_l$.

This provides the means to test whether a measurement system possesses the interval property, for if two pairs of objects are assigned numbers equally distant on the number scale, then it must be assumed that the objects are equally different in the real world. For example, in order for the first test in a statistics class to possess the interval property, it must be true that two students making scores of 23 and 28 respectively must reflect the same change in knowledge of statistics as two students making scores of 30 and 35.

The property of intervals is critical in terms of the ability to meaningfully use the mathematical operations "+" and "-". To the extent to which the property of intervals is not satisfied, any statistic that is produced by adding or subtracting numbers will be in error.

Rational Zero

A measurement system possesses a rational zero if an object that has none of the attribute in question is assigned the number zero by the system of rules. The object does not need to really exist in the "real world", as it is somewhat difficult to visualize a "man with no height". The requirement for a rational zero is this: if objects with none of the attribute did exist would they be given the value zero. Defining O0 as the object with none of the attribute in question, the definition of a rational zero becomes:

The property of rational zero exists if $M(O_0) = 0$.

The property of rational zero is necessary for ratios between numbers to be meaningful. Only in a measurement system with a rational zero would it make sense to argue that a person with a score of 30 has twice as much of the attribute as a person with a score of 15. In many application of statistics this property is not necessary to make meaningful inferences.

Level of Measurement

The level of measurement of a variable in mathematics and statistics describes how much information the numbers associated with the variable contain. Different mathematical operations on variables are possible, depending on the level at which a variable is measured. In statistics, the kinds of descriptive statistics and significance tests that are appropriate depend on the level of measurement of the variables concerned.

Four levels of measurement are usually recognized:

Nominal measurement. The numbers are names or labels. They can and often are replaced by verbal names. If two entities have the same number associated with them, they belong to the same category, and that is the only significance that they have. The only comparisons that can be made between variable values are equality and inequality. There are no "less than" or "greater than" relations among them, nor operations such as addition or subtraction. Examples include: the international telephone code for a country, the numbers on the shirts of players in a sports team, or the number of a bus. The only kind of measure of central tendency is the mode. Information entropy is available as a measure of statistical dispersion, but no notion of standard deviation or the like exists. Variables that are measured only nominally are also called categorical variables.

Ordinal measurement. The numbers have all the features of nominal measures and also represent the rank order (1st, 2nd, 3rd etc) of the entities measured. The numbers are ordinals. Comparisons of greater and less can be made, in addition to equality and inequality. However operations such as conventional addition and subtraction are still without meaning. A physical example is the Mohs scale of mineral hardness. Another example is the results of a horse race; which horses arrived first, second, third, etc. are reported, but the time intervals between the horses are not reported. Most measurement in psychology and other social sciences is at the ordinal level; for example attitudes and IQ are only measured at the ordinal level. If customers surveyed report preferring chocolate- to vanilla-flavored ice cream, the data are of this kind. The central tendency of a distribution an ordinally measured variable can be represented by its mode or its median; the latter will give more information. Variables measured at the ordinal level are referred to as ordinal variables or rank variables.

Interval measurement. The numbers have all the features of ordinal measurement and also are separated by the same interval. In this case, differences between arbitrary pairs of numbers can be meaningfully compared. Operations such as addition and subtraction are therefore meaningful. However, the zero point on the scale is arbitrary, and ratios between numbers on the scale are not meaningful, so operations such as multiplication and division cannot be carried out. On the other hand, negative values on the scale can be used. An example is the year date in many calendars. The central tendency of a distribution a variable measured at the interval level can be represented by its mode, its median or its arithmetic mean; the mean will give most information. Variables measured at the interval level are referred to as interval variables, or sometimes as scaled variables, though the latter usage is not obvious and is not recommended.

Ratio measurement. The numbers have all the features of interval measurement and also have meaningful ratios between arbitrary pairs of numbers. Operations such as multiplication and division are therefore meaningful. The zero value on a ratio scale is non-arbtrary. Most physical quantities, such as mass, length or energy are measured on ratio scales; so is temperature when it is measured in kelvins, i.e. relative to absolute zero. The central tendency of a distribution an variable measured at the interval level can be represented by its mode, its median, its arithmetic mean, or its geometric mean; however as with an interval scale, the arithmetic mean will give the most useful information. Variables measured at the interval level are referred to as ratio variables.

Interval and/or ratio measurement are sometimes referred to as "true measurement", though this usage reflects a lack of understanding of the uses of
ordinal measurement. However, it is only quantities measured on ratio scales
that can correctly be said to have units of measurement.

There is some controversy in behavioral sciences over whether the mean is
meaningful for ordinal measurement. Mathematically it is not, but some
behavioral scientists use it anyway. This is often justified on the basis that ordinal
scales in behavioral science are really somewhere between true ordinal and interval
scales—although the interval difference between two ordinal ranks is not constant, it is often of the same order of magnitude. Thus, some argue, that so long as
the unknown interval difference between ordinal scale ranks is not too variable,
interval scale statistics such as means can meaningfully be used on ordinal scale
variables.

Reliability and Validity

All measurements are subject to error. This means that one is never able to quote
an exact value for a measured physical quantity. If the height of a tree is estimated
to lie somewhere between 38.5 and 39.5 m, then the result should be quoted as
39 m (3.9 x 10). Such a measurement is said to have been made to two significant
digits.

It is important that the correct number of significant digits is reported in any
measurement—a long string of digits that has no significance is misleading as it
indicates a very precise measurement (or a very small error). Meaningless digits
are particularly liable to arise from a series of calculations. To avoid confusion,
rules for determining (and reporting) the numbers of significant digits have been
developed.

Measurement in Marketing Research

The results of marketing research can inform marketing decisions such as in
concept/product testing, market segmentation, competitive analysis, customer
satisfaction studies, etc. and illustrates the need for measurement.

Not all of what researchers do involves measurement. Researchers are interested
in generating information, which leads to knowledge, which leads to better decisions. Sometimes that information is in the form of insights from exploratory

research studies such as focus groups, in-depth interviews, projective research, and similar methods. For these techniques we are generating information, but we are not 'assigning numbers to objects,' so we rare not 'measuring.' As we have said before, information does not have to have numbers attached to it to have value, and we are dangerously oversimplifying our analysis when we favor information with numbers over that without, simply because it has the appearance of being 'hard evidence'.

The 'rules for assigning numbers' will be discussed in greater depth in this chapter, but we should note here that those rules exist so that we can be more scientific in our measures, and can place more confidence in the numbers that those rules help generate. We want to make decisions that are grounded in information that we believe correctly represent reality. This means the assignment of numbers should map the empirical nature isomorphically (i.e. on a 'one-to-one' basis).

For example, if we assign the number '5 lbs' to represent the weight of an object, we want to make sure that weight is 5 lbs and not 8 lbs or 3 lbs. Using a carefully calibrated scale is how we ensure in this example that we have correctly measured the item's weight—assigned numbers to the object to accurately represent the quantity of its attribute of weight. The mundane quality of this example disappears when we find ourselves confronted with the need to measure variables of interest to marketers such as intentions, attitudes, perceptions, etc. How can we be sure that the number '4' correctly captures the intensity with which a respondent holds an intention, for example? We will devote further discussion to the ways of ensuring good measures in our research.

The definition states that we attach numbers to the attributes of an object and not to the object itself. Fore example, we cannot measure the quantity of what you are now holding in your hand. There is no scale for measuring the amount of 'bookness' in a book. We can, however, measure the attributes of a book—its weight, dimensions in inches, number of pages, and so forth. We can even measure qualities less obvious such as its stature as great literature or its educational value; but, as described in point number 2, the rules for assigning numbers to those attributes will involve different measuring devices than those used to measure its physical properties. This caveat also holds true for the measurement of variables of interest to marketers.

We measure a consumer's attitudes, income, brand loyalty, etc., instead of measuring the consumer. In some cases, such as attitudes, we go a step further and measure the subcomponents of the variable. Attitudes, for example, are said to consist to ensure we have captured the essence of how strong one's attitude was toward an object. For example, if we are to claim we have measured a parent's attitude toward a new product concept for a child's fruit drink, we need to measure beliefs and knowledge (the cognitive component of attitudes), how positive or negative he or she feels about the concept (the affective component), and the parent's predisposition to behave toward the product (the conative component).

Scientists in the physical sciences such as physics, chemistry, and biology have something of an advantage over behavioral scientists because the things they are interested in measuring have a physical reality, and the devices used to measure these things can be physically calibrated. 'Good measures' are generated by carefully calibrating the measuring devices (e.g., micrometers, weight scales, etc.). Behavioral scientists, such as marketing researchers, cannot see or feel those things of interest to them (e.g. perceptions, intentions, brand loyalty, attitudes, etc.), and so must find ways of determining if the process they use to attach numbers is trustworthy in order to know if the numbers resulting from that weight of a chemical is what a carefully calibrated scales says it is, the marketing researcher can trust that he or she has obtained a good measure of intent to purchase only by having faith in the measurement process used to attach numbers to that intention. There is no way of comparing the numbers on the intention scale to a standardized measure for intentions the way a chemist can check the measures of weight against a standardized scale for weight. We trust the numbers because we trust the process used to attach those numbers.

The Process of Measurement

Information gained from conducting marketing research contributes to better decision making by reducing risk, which can happen only if researchers are able to collect information that accurately represents the phenomenon under study. When it is appropriate to measure that phenomenon, that is, attach numbers to reflect the amount of an attribute inherent in that object of interest, then we must try to ensure that the process we use to take those measures is a 'good' process. We have nothing to compare those numbers to determine if they are 'good' numbers, so we make sure the process is trustworthy and can indeed reduce the risk of decision marking. The following process can help generate good measures.

Step 1: Determine the Construct(s) of interest

Constructs are abstract 'constructions' (hence, the name) that are of interest to researchers. Some examples of constructs of interest to marketing researchers are customer satisfaction, heavy users, channel conflict, brand loyalty, marketing orientation, etc. These constructs are typical of the type of constructions of interest to marketers—they have no tangible reality apart from our defining them (unlike, for example, a biologist's plant), and we define them and study them because we need to understand them in order to market decisions based on that understanding (e.g., changing our policies on return of purchases to increase customer satisfaction). Because they cannot see customer satisfaction, but we can indirectly observe it by asking customers a series of questions that we believe reveal how satisfied customers are with our firm in specific areas. As an example of measuring a construct we will use 'marketing orientation'—a core construct of the marketing discipline.

Step 2: Specify the Construct's Domain

We must take care that we are accurately capturing what should be included in the definition of that contact. We previously mentioned that the tricomponent model indicates that an attitude contains in its domain cognitive, affective, and conative components. Social scientists have studied the construct 'attitude' over many years and have generally agreed that its domain includes these three components. We specify a construct's domain by providing a constitutive definition for the construct. A constitutive definition defines a construct by using other constructs to identify conceptual boundaries, showing how it is discernable for mother similar but different constructs. Consider the differences in the constitutive definitions for the following related, but different, constructs:

Step 3: Establish Operational Definitions

The constitutive definition makes it possible to better define the construct's domain by use of an operational definition. An operational definition indicates what observable attributes of the construct will be measured and the process that will be used to attach numbers to those attributes so as to represent the quantity of the attributes.

We need to establish operational definitions of our constructs to move them from the world of abstract concepts into the empirical world where we can measure them. Marketing orientation remains an abstract concept until we say exactly what its attributes are and how, specifically, we intend to measure those attributes.

Step 4: Collect Data to Test Measures

In this step we use our operationalized measures to collect data from our target population. We need this data to help us determine if we are on the right track with our operationalized measures. That is, have we done a good job in developing the operational definitions and measuring processes so that they accurately represent our constructs of interest? As was mentioned before, since we have no standardized measures that can be calibrated to give us accurate data, such as a chemist using a carefully calibrated weight scale, we must use data to help us determine if the methods used to collect that data were 'good'. If the process of measurement is good the results of the process will also be assumed to be good. 'Collecting data' in the previous two examples would consist of using the questionnaires to collect responses from the target populations (hospital administrators in the first example, executives at manufacturing firms in the second).

Step 5: Purify the Measures

In step 5 we use the data collected in Step 4 to determine which items in our original list of operationalized items have 'made the cut'. Some items we thought would be good ways to operationalize our abstract constructs may not be as good as we thought. We can determine which item list by conducting reliability tests. We will discuss reliability in greater detail later in this chapter, but suffice it to say for now that we are using some statistical procedures to help identify which item statements 'hang together' as a set, capturing the various aspects of the construct's attributes we were seeking to measure in our operationalizations.

Step 6: Conduct Validity Tests

Once we have purified the scale by eliminating item statements that fail to pass our reliability test we are ready to conduct another test to determine how much faith we will place in the results of our research. Here we are testing for validity— did we actually measure what we were trying to measure? Validity will also be discussed in greater depth later in this chapter. Here, we should merely make note of the need to determine how successful we were in establishing measures that did correctly reflect the quantities of those attributes of our constructs of interest (e.g. Did we, in fact, accurately measure the degree to which an organization was marketing oriented?).

Step 7: Analyze Research Findings

If we have successfully developed measures that are reliable (Step 5) and valid (Step 6) we are now ready to analyze our data to achieve the objectives of our research study: answer research questions, test hypotheses, check for cause and effect relationships, describe the extent to which a population behaves in a specific manner, etc. A report can then be written that states the results of the research.

Commentary on the Measurement Process

Note that in this seven-step process data are actually analyzed two different ways. In Steps 5 and 6 data are being analyzed not to determine what are the findings of the research itself (i.e., not to obtain answers to the research questions), but rather to determine if the process used to collect the data generated results which can be trusted—that is, did the process generate reliable, valid information. Both of these measurements of 'data trustworthiness' are matters of degree instead of binary yes or no conclusions. We determine the degree of reliability and validity rather than determining the data is or is not reliable or valid. Once we have established degree of reliability and validity we are in a better position to know how secure we can be in our research conclusions when we analyze the same data in Step 7 to achieve that purpose of doing the research study itself.

We should also point out that some measurement processes suggest collecting data twice—once to determine which item statements are reliable (i.e., after Step 4), then again after unreliable item statements have been eliminated (i.e., between Steps 4 and 5), performing reliability and validity tests on the second set of data, followed by analysis of the data for research findings (Step 7).

Now a reality check: Do all or most marketing research studies actually follow a measurement process similar to the seven step process outlined here? Well, yes and no. Marketing scholars doing research on topics of interest to the discipline of marketing (such as 'Does being marketing oriented increase a firm's profit?'), would have to do something like this process or they might not get their research results published! However, applied marketing-research studies, such as described in this text, are less vigilant in conducting such measurement processes. It should be obvious that all researchers are concerned whether or not they have measures that can be trusted before drawing conclusions and making decisions based on research findings. Therefore, attention to issues of construct domain, proper operational definitions, appropriate data-collection methods, and reliability and validity checks are efforts intended to generate data that accurately represents the object of the research and can lead to better decisions.

What is to be Measured

There are many different types of measures used in marketing research. However, most measures fall into one of the following three categories:

1. States of being—age, sex, income, education, etc.
2. Behavior—purchase, patterns, brand loyalty, etc.
3. States of mind—attitudes, preferences, personality, etc.

The criterion for selecting what to measure is based on our knowledge or expectation that what we want to measure will provide insight into or help solve the marketing decision problem for which data are being collected. Thus, the relevant measures for any study are based on the research objectives, which indicate the types of information needed.

The research objectives indicate the concepts (constructs) that must be measured. For example, customer satisfaction, store loyalty, and sales performance are all concepts that relate to marketing problems. However, most concepts can be measured in more than one way. Store loyalty, for example, could be measured by: (1) the number of times a store is visited, (2) the proportion of purchases made at a store, or (3) shopping at a particular store first. We develop operational definitions for two types of variables: discrete and continuous.

Discrete variables are those that can be identified, separated into entities, and counted. The number of children in a family is an example of a discrete variable. Although the average may be 3.5, a given family would have 1,2,3, or 4 more children, but not 3.5.

Continuous variables may take on any value. As a simple rule, if a third value can fall between the two other values, the variable is continuous. It can take on an infinite number of values within some specified range. Temperature, distance, and time are continuous variables, and each can be measured to finer and finer degrees of accuracy. Frequently, continuous variables are rounded and converted to discrete variables expressed in convenient units such as degrees, miles and minutes.

Who is to be Measured

The question of the object of the measurement process may appear to have obvious answers: people, stores, or geographic areas. However, more thoughtful answers would reveal a multiplicity of possible objects to be measured.

For example, study of martial roles in decision processes yielded four distinctively different perceptions of the role of the husband and wife. In essence, the role played by each person varied with the product being purchased. The husband was dominant in the purchase of life insurance, the wife was dominant in food and kitchenware purchases. They tended to share equal roles in purchasing housing, vacations and living room furniture, and to be autonomic or independent in the purchase of the husband's clothing and nonprescription drugs. Another study revealed that both teenage boys and girls play an important role in the family's purchase of grocery items, especially where working mothers or single parents were present. Thus, collecting data from the 'decision maker' does not always represent an obvious choice of respondent.

The buying-center concept used in understanding organizational buying patterns provides a useful framework for other consumer and industrial purchasers. A buying center consists of everyone involved in a buying action.

Buying-center participants play different roles. These roles must be identified and understood to select the type of respondents to be measured in a research project. These roles are:

1. User—hose who actually use the product
2. Gatekeepers—hose who control the flow of information or access to decision makers.
3. Influencers—those who influence the choice of product or supplier by providing information.
4. Deciders—those who actually make the choice of product and/or supplier
5. Buyers—those who actually complete the exchange process for a family or organization.

The major point of this discussion is to emphasize the need to judiciously select the respondents, stores, areas—i.e., the 'who' to be measured. If we ask questions of the wrong people, we will still get answers; they will not be meaningful and could even be misleading.

The choice of what parameters or variables to measure is not trivial. Considerable thought and planning are needed to ensure that time, effort and money are not wasted in measuring unimportant items. It is important that the measurements made are:

- appropriate to the questions that need to be answered,
- related to what is already known about the object to be measured,
- possible with the resources available.

Notes and References

[1] S.S. Stevens, Mathematics, Mesurement and Psychophysics, Handbook of Experimental Psychology, pages 1-49. J. Wiley, New York, 1951.

Chapter 2

Integration of Market Research

In most companies, the market research department so-called strategic planning department in some global companies is an important function reporting directly to the core management panel such as CEO in headquarter instead of marketing department. It burdens the tremendous and significant undertaking of strategic planning for the company operation.

To optimize the working effectiveness, market research staff must position themselves well in the organization and to authorize themselves right to access to any operating function of the company freely including design engineers, upper management, salespeople, product managers, and sales managers. Market research can have a positive impact on all functions of the company, so its connection with every part of the organization should not be hindered.

Having conducted primary market research on both end-users and competitors, the market research manager now possesses a tremendous amount of invaluable business intelligence. Being aware of this, upper management becomes increasingly eager to examine these findings and collaborate directly with the research department.

The majority of companies fail at the integration stage. They do not hire people with awareness of the necessity to incorporate the market research process into the broad corporate activities. Therefore, the market research function can only get evolved into a very limited functions with little real significance in the company operation strategy.

Chart 2.1 Marketing integration

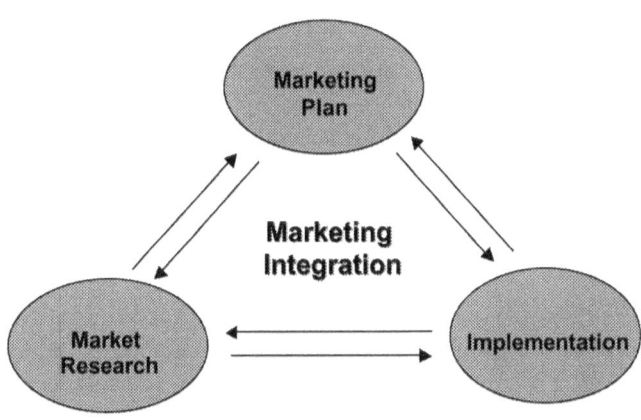

One prestigious global logistics company has intimated in one round meeting with Frost & Sullivan "We can make pragmatic strategies by ourselves since most of us are experienced logistics expert..." This is partly true. Market research is regarded as an invaluable resource premised for marketing plan. Market analysts pry into the problem with insightful marketing perspective which generates knowledge platform of certain market to shepherd the decision makers. Then the strategies will be developed based on the repository of market resource. The marketing interface is created during the follow-up action and decision implementation after strategy establishment for sales and manufacturing. New problems come up with encountered difficulties in operation when the management panel was obsessed with natural-ties such as market downturn. The problems are transferred to market research function for further perception. Marketing integration is an interactive process which needs resonations from three segments: market research, marketing plan, and implementation. These three components work independently with effective feedbacks to each other and strong ties linking with each other.

Sales & Marketing

A carefully crafted combination of sales and marketing is vital for successful business growth. "Selling" or making sales consists of interpersonal interaction of one-on-one meetings, telephone calls and networking that you engage in with prospects and customers. "marketing" encompasses programs businesses use to reach and persuade prospects, including advertising, public relations, direct mail and more.

Prospects normally move through the sales cycle from cold to warm, and then finally hot there they're ready to "close" and become clients or customers. Throughout the sales cycle, it will take multiple contacts using both sales and marketing to move prospects to the next level. To build a successful business, you must develop a program that combines sales and marketing and reaches out to prospects in all three stages old, warm or hot on an ongoing basis.

What does market research do between marketing and sales? How to piggyback the market research on the relationship between marketing and sales? Market research play vital role in combing sales and marketing which is the key connection between these two. Intriguingly, the fact sometimes skews in the favor of negative effect. One Korean leading chemical company came to Frost & Sullivan for marketing research. The marketing strategy department brought sales team into the discussion on the project. Superficially it is part of helpful to the research. But the unpredicted problems came out later in the meeting. The sales team emphasized on the importance of contact points and feasible approach to achieve sales revenue instead of market measurements and strategic recommendation.

To incorporate sales with market research is undoubtedly right, but not right at any stage. The facing problem is when and how to incorporate market research into sales and marketing. The three stages of market research integration is illustrated in Chart 2.2. The initial stage is the cross point between marketing and sales. Market research is defined to have little connection with marketing and sales. The rational time for the real integration is at the stage of marketing plan. The marketing strategies generate from the in-depth data analysis of market research and prepared by both marketing and sales team collaborating with reach team or external consulting companies with even far-lung technological knowledge. At that stage, companies attempt to build actionable strategies to offer their customers complete solutions instead of stand-alone products and services, they need to obtain a better understanding of the myriad, subtle and often unarticulated needs of customers with the help of market research. In the third stage, the implementation is a broad interaction between marketing and sales. Two sides fully cooperate in all walks of strategic implementation such as product promotion and position.

Chart 2.2 Integration of market research into sales and marketing

Market Research	Marketing Plan	Implementation
Marketing — Sales	Marketing — Sales	Marketing — Sales

Communication

Communication bridges the market research and marketing between clients and research suppliers which is a key skill of marketers and effective marketing researchers. The marketing research professional who understands managerial decision-making and can design good research also needs to possess effective communication skills to ensure the research has the proper influence. The functions of communication in market research are transition from analysis of data, formation of information, development of conclusions, development of recommendations etc.

The market research process does not end at the presentation stage. A well incorporated, properly functioning market research department will continue to discuss research findings. It will also follow up on implementation with key decision makers, ensuring that the implications of the market information are understood and agreements on action plans for the future are accepted.

The true effectiveness of the market research activity can only be measured if communication is taken on the information, analysis, and recommendations between the research department and marketing department.

The lack of communication on an action plan is a major flaw in the role of market research. Market research will not become a profitable business investment until effective communication is established.

Chapter 3

Market General

Market general provides a snapshot of defined market to offer parishioners a market qualification by measurement. Some measures such as market size are essential and sensitive to the investors to make decisions on investment. Some measures can be used to gauge the company growth such as market growth rate. Market general is the first step in marketing research, especially for industrial products.

This chapter anatomizes the frequently used market measures as follows:

- Market environment
- Market age
- Market size
- Market growth rate
- Market share
- Market potential
- Market concentration
- Market saturation
- Market attractiveness
- Replacement rate

Market Environment

Definition

Industries are embedded in a wider macroenvironment that can significantly impact the competitiveness of industries and the companies within industries. The starting point of any strategic analysis is some form of environmental analysis. To perform an environmental analysis, market researchers must understand the basic structures of marketing environments.

The marketing environment consists of actors and forces outside the organization that affect management's ability to build and maintain relationships with target customers. It is a interactive relationship between actors. Environment offers both opportunities and threats to all actors. Marketing intelligence and research are used to collect information about the environment to provide market insights to the decision makers to help them build effective operation strategy.

The marketing environment can be commonly divided into three layers: internal environment, microenvironment and macroenvironment. The internal environment includes the forces that operate inside the organization with specific implications for managing organizational performance. The microenvironment contains actors close to the company that affect its ability to serve its customers; the macroenvironment includes larger societal forces that affect the microenvironment which are considered to be beyond the control of the organization.

■ Internal environment

Internal environment is the areas inside a company which affects the marketing department's planning strategies. All departments must "think consumer" and work together to provide superior customer value and satisfaction. The aspects of internal environment (production, marketing, etc.) collectively define both trouble spots that need strengthening and core competencies that the company can nurture and build. By systematically examining its internal activities the company can better appreciate how each activity might add value or contribute significantly to shaping an effective strategy.

■ Microenvironment

The microenvironment, sometimes termed the competitive or market environment, is that level of the macroenvironment with components that normally have relatively specific and immediate implications for managing the organization.

The major actors in microenvironment are company, suppliers (such as capital providers or labor), marketing intermediaries, customers, competitors, and publics. The microenvironment, unlike the macroenvironment, can be controlled or influenced, at least to some extent, by individual companies. Also unlike the macroenviroment, analysis at this level is firm specific.

- Suppliers:

  To provide resources needed (such as capital, raw materials, labor etc) to produce goods and services. Most marketers treat suppliers like partners which is important component in value chain analysis.

- Marketing Intermediaries:

  To help the company promote, sell, and distribute its goods to final buyers which includes resellers, physical distribution firms, marketing services agencies, financial intermediaries etc.

- Customers:

  It has five types of customers that purchase a company's goods and services including: individual consumer, business, reseller, government, international.

- Competitors:

  Those who serve a target market with products and services that are viewed by consumers as being reasonable substitutes.

- Publics:

  Group that has an interest in or impact on an organization's ability to achieve its objectives. There are several types of publics: financial, media, government, citizen-action etc.

■ Macroenvironment

The macroenvironment is that level of an organization's environment that is broad in scope and has long-term implications for firms. These are usually understood to be beyond the direct influence or primary control of any single organization which includes demographic, economic, natural, technological, political, culture.

Methods of Measurements

To make the task of environment analysis more meaningful, the macroenvironment has to be broken down into more homogeneous and manageable subcategories. One effective subcategorization is known as the PEST categorization system. The

PEST categorization, also sometimes called PESTE, STEP, STEEP or PESTLE, looks at the external business environment. In fact, it would be better to call this kind of analysis—a business environmental analysis, but the acronym PEST/PESTE/PESTLE/STEP/STEEP is easy to remember and so has stuck. The differences for all full names of acronyms are illustrated in Figure 3.1. PESTLE is the most comprehensive categorization.

Figure 3.1 Market Environment: Business Environmental Analysis Acronyms

Acronym	Full Name
PEST	Political, Economic, Sociocultural and Technological
PESTE	Political, Economic, Sociocultural, Technological and Environmental
PESTLE	Political, Economic, Sociocultural, Technological, Legal and Environmental
STEP	Sociocultural, Technological, Economic and Political,
STEEP	Sociocultural, Technological, Economic, Environmental, and Political,

The business environmental analysis examines the impact of each of these factors (and their interplay with each other) on the business. The results can then be used to take advantage of opportunities and to make contingency plans for threats when preparing business and strategic plans.

Each environmental factor needs to be analyzed as they all play a part in determining the overall business environment. PEST analysis, as an example, can be conducted as follows:

■ Political

When looking at political factors the impact of any political or legislative changes should be considered that could affect business operation. If the company is operating in more than one country then each country needs to be investigated in turn. Political factors include aspects such as laws on maternity rights, data protection and even environmental policy: these three examples alone have an on impact employment terms, information access, product specification and business processes in many businesses globally.

■ Economic

Obviously politicians don't operate in a vacuum, and many political changes result from changes in the economy or in social and cultural mores, for example. Thus although tax rates are generally decided by politicians, tax decisions generally also include economic considerations such as what is the state of the economy. In Europe, the politicians drove the introduction of the euro currency but the impacts include economic factors: cross-border pricing, European interest rates, bank charges, price transparency and so on. Other economic factors include exchange rates, inflation levels, income growth, debt & saving levels (which impact available money) and consumer & business confidence. There can also be narrow industry measures that become important. Issues such as the availability of skilled labour or raw-material costs can impact industries in different ways.

- Sociocultural

  All the various PEST factors are governed by the sociocultural factors. These are the elements that build society. Social factors influence people's choices and include societal beliefs, values and attitudes. So understanding changes in this area can be crucial, as they lead to political and societal change. Demographic changes and consumer views on the product & industry needs to be considered; environmental issues, especially if the product involves hazardous or potentially damaging production processes; lifestyle changes and attitudes to health, wealth age (children, the elderly, etc.), gender, work and leisure. Added complications when looking at social and cultural factors are differences in ethnic and social groups. Not all groups have the same attitudes and this influences how they view various products and services.

- Technological

  Advances in technology can have a major impact on business success, with companies that fail to keep up often going out of business. Technological change also affects political and economic aspects, and plays a part in how people view their world. Just as one example, the Internet has had a major influence on the ways consumers and businesses research and purchase products. Whereas ten or even five years ago, it was rare for consumers to consider cross-border purchases this is now becoming common via services such as eBay, with the result that even small businesses can now serve a global market. Politicians are still coming to grips with the tax issues involved. Meanwhile the music industry has still not found an effective solution to the threat posed by the successors to Napster. Environmental factors to consider here include the impact of climate change: water and winter fuel costs could change dramatically if the world warms by only a couple of degrees.

Figure 3.2 has listed some specified key considerations can be made in PEST analysis.

Figure 3.2 Market Environment: Key Consideration in PEST Analysis

Political	Economic	Sociacultural	Technological
Environmental regulation and protection	Economic growth (overall by industry setor)	Income distribution (change in distribution of disposable income)	Government spending on research.
Taxation (corporate consumer)	Monetary policy (interest rates)	Demographics (age structure of the population, gender, family size and composition; changing nature of occupations)	Government and industry focus on technological effort
International trade regulation	Government spending (overall level, specific spending priorities)	Labor/social mobility	New discovery and development
Customer protection	Policy towards employment (Minimun wage, unemployment benefits, grants)	Lifestyle changes (eg. home working, single households)	Speed of technology transfer
Environmental law	Taxation (impact on customer disposable income, incentive to invest in capital equipment, corporation tax rates)	Attitudes to work and leisure	Rate of technological obsolescence
Government organization/attitude	Exchange rate (effect on demand of overseas customers; effect on cost of imported components)	Education	Energy use and costs
Competition regulation	Inflation (effect on coast and selling prices)	Fashion and fads	Change in material science.

Case Study: Marketing Macroenvironment Anatomy of China

An outside-inside view has been repeatedly highlighted by excellent companies since the marketing environment is constantly spinning out new opportunities and threats. Companies recognize the vital importance of continuously monitoring and adapting to the changing environment. Successful companies are those that can recognize and respond profitably to unmet needs and trends in the macroenvironment. Unmet needs always exist in any regional or segmented marketplace, especially in the world most populous country with wonder, enigma, opportunities and threats—China.

Financial Times (24 June 2004, pp.14) reports that the Chinese economy is nothing short of an economic miracle. With a current GDP of $ 1,463 billion, it already ranks second in Asia after Japan, though globally lagging behind the USA, Japan, Germany, UK, France and Italy. But with growth rates of 9.1% in 2003 and 9.8% in the first quarter of 2004, China is hoping to surpass the UK in 2005/06 and Germany by 2015. This would place China in third place in the global GDP league, behind the USA and Japan. With its 1.4 billion population, China offers both reserves of cheap labor and of potential demand. As such, China is both a prolific producer and voracious consumer of goods. Many of the recent price increases—be they for copper, zinc or steel—have been traced to China's door by inducing global shortage. In 2003, China used 27% of the world's steel output, 31% of its coal and 40% of its cement. Not only is China the workshop of the world, accounting for 7% of global manufacturing output, it already offers a sizeable domestic market. Sales of steel and machine tools are higher than anywhere else in the world, as are sales of personal computers. It is already the world's biggest market for mobile phones, the second largest electricity transmission equipment and the fourth biggest for cars and trucks.

China becomes the nervous leader of world economy, thus it is incumbent upon marketers to understand the market dynamics and pry into the trends and megatrends of Chinese market. Marketing opportunities are always found by identifying opportunities.

- Political factor

Current China is in the social transformation period experiencing not only system change from conventional political economic system to market-oriented economic system, but also technology innovation, especially the network technology development. So far, Chinese people still concentrate on the benefits of the system transformation to the political stabilization, whereas the side effect of technology innovation to political stabilization is always kept aside ignorantly. Virtually information communication can leverage the social stability:

The political information transparency in China shall be improved to upraise the publicity of political decision, to eliminate political mysteries, to throttle political hearsay, to solicit public opinion. China is still in the initiation period of information communication channel management and need to enhance international cooperation with other countries to improve the management level. To head in this way, Chinese authorities have shown great technical ability to block offending websites and junk email to sustain the political and social stability.

■ Economic factor

With income level climbing up, exotic furlough, cell phone and computer becomes new consuming highlights to the Chinese. The retail market is the biggest beneficiary enjoying 13.1% increase (July–Aug. 2004). Bloomberg News (15 Sept. 2004) reports that the sales revenue of Chinese retail market continued soaring up staggeringly by 424 billion Renminbi (China Yuan) in August this year. During the first eight months of this year the sales revenue of retail market has augmented by 12.9% and achieved 3,370 billion Renminbi (China Yuan).

The average income of Chinese people has outpaced $ 1,000 which will be doubled by 2015 and is forecasted to achieve 20% even 40% of American average in 2030. In the most modern city of China—Shanghai, the average annual disposal income has outstripped $890. The income ascending in Beijing and Shanghai has attracted much attention from foreign investors gloabally. Meanwhile, fear of overheating has already resulted in administrative measures to curb the investment growth; the pertinent stunning peril is believed to be circumvented by increasing social consumption.

The expected rational growth of Chinese economy will rely more on internal demands. According to statistics, in the first half year, the average disposal income of urban population (approximately 1/3 of total) in China has reached $ 582 with growth rate 12%. Asian biggest Air-tickets service company Abacus International reports that 2% of Chinese people have exotic travel experience and Chinese exotic tourism surges by 15-20% each year. Japanese biggest retail baron Aeon has announced to set up 100 retail stores in China and the first one will be expected to put into operation by the end of 2004. Likewise, the world second largest luxury manufacturer Richmond has announced to increase the number of its chain stores in China by 1/3 by 2006 to satisfy the customer demand of watch, bag, pen etc.

Reports say that the sales revenue of retail market in Chinese township area increased by 14% in August 2004 and reached 282 billion Renminbi (China Yuan); that in rural area also climbed up by 11% and arrived at 144 billion Renminbi (China Yuan). The sales revenue of food increased by 28%, partly because the food price has moved up by 14%.

In the mean time, with total number of consumer cars ascending and oil price swinging up, the sales revenue of petrol gas and related products has soared a staggering increase by 49%. The number of urban consumer cars doubled in the first half year and reached the level of 2 cars per 100 families averagely which is still far lagging behind of US level of 2 cars per family.

Recently, the fervent purchase passion in automotive market has cooled down. One reason is that Chinese administrative has imposed restrictions on consumer car loans in consideration of economic soft landing; the other reason is the consumers hold to expect the car price further decline. Because of the inventory hyperinflation from auto makers side, the price decreased by 13%.

Beijing Hyundai can not reach the production goal of this year 0.15 million. Taiwanese auto maker—China Motor has intimated that can not achieve the profitability goal of this year because of current weak purchasing power in China. In the perspective of cost increase and sales downturn, Morgan Stanley has reduced the investment evaluation rating of Chinese automotive industry from 'interposition' to 'prudence'.

In addition, the sales revenue of telecommunication equipments increased by 39%, that of home furnishings ascended by 34%, however that of electrical appliances has climbed up by 1.3%.

■ Socialculture factor

White paper 'China 21st Century Population and Development' promulgated by Chinese State Council in 2000, as a guideline of the development trend of Chinese population, intimates that the aim of Chinese population controls in the future is as follows: the total population will be controlled at 1.3 billion in 2005 and 1.4 billion in 2010. This figure will reach the peak of 1.5-1.6 billion approximately in 2030. It is well-accepted that 1.6 billion is the upper line of Chinese population. Chinese population undergoes lukewarmly gentle growth and will reverse to negative eventually under the effect of long term pragmatic implementation of One-child Policy.

Currently, China faces five essential population problems:

- *Low population quality.* From 1990's, the quality of Chinese population continuously increases which can be interpreted by illiterate ratio: the illiterate ratio of Chinese population in 1990 is 22.21% which plummeted to 15.41% in 1999 with average decreasing rate 0.7%. In spite of this, education level of Chinese population is still very low. The average education length of Chinese people is 7.85 year on par with the level of America 100 years ago. Statistics shows that only 4.63% of age 25-64 group holds college diploma or above which is equivalent to 1/4 of EU level in 1999.

  To eliminate illiterates scoops the first priority in Chinese education plan. Central government has poured profuse Renmingbi (China Yuan) into rural area with intention to reconstruct the education environment and situation. However, unbalanced regional economic development incommodes education development. Thousands of education founds are embezzled to prod and coincide with overheating economic development.

  Chinese people have ambition and they crave knowledge. Young generation has strong aspiration to study aboard. Statistics shows that from 1987 to 2003 the total number of Chinese overseas students abroad amounts to 0.7 million which has soared an astonishing increase since 1998. The number of self-founded students in 1998 is 11,000, whereas the number in 2002 is 117,000 and 11 times higher than 1998.

  The study-abroad service market has shaped up in China already brewing large business opportunity to investors. Currently China has 228 study-abroad service agencies helping students who are striving for studying abroad. Their work is to prepare application documents to university and for visa, some agencies even have capability to arrange overseas accommodations for students. The price for such service is prohibitive and much higher than that in US and EU and seems unaffordable to most Chinese people, but this market is still unbelievably profoundly lucrative as well known.

- *Large population shifts.* In 2000, 0.11 billion people moved from rural area to urban area. The population urbanization rate is accelerating by 1% annually before 2020 that brings much pressure to economic development.

- *Sex ratio of birth further lopsided.* The Fifth Population Census (2000) shows the male to female ratio of birth is 117:100, that of ethnic minority group is higher as 130:100. Such high ratio will cause new social problem.

- *Growing trend of AIDS.* There exist approximately 0.84 million reported patients with AIDS infection in China in 2003 at the stake of diffusing from high-risk group to generic group. If appropriate measures are not adopted, the total infected number will surge up to 10 million in 2010.

■ Technological factor

The most dramatic force shaping people's lives is technology. Technology has released such wonders as penicillin, open-heart surgery, and birth-control pill. The economy's growth rate is affected by how many major new technologies are discovered.

In China, R&D does not rein the prominence which can be judged from R&D budgets. Although the absolute total investment of R&D is swinging up by approximately 20% each year and has reached $15 billion on par with 1/5 of total R&D expenditure of US, the ratio of R&D investment in GDP is still exceedingly low remaining at lower than 1%, in comparison with 2.3-2.9% of US, Japan and Germany. The financial sources of R&D expenditure in China consist of government technology subsidy, enterprises investment, and bank technology loan. The share of self-founding, namely enterprises investment, has been increasing dramatically these years. But current total R&D investment still can not satisfy the demand of rapid economic development.

In the meantime, China is short of high tech experts and specialists. Out of one thousand labors the number of R&D scientists and engineers is only 0.7 in China, but 7.3 in US, 7.9 in Japan, 6.2 in Germany which demonstrates the intractable technology gap between developed countries and China.

Nevertheless, China has own strategic consideration to tackle this tough problem. During the evolvement from export destination to the world largest manufacturing site, China strives to absorb advanced technologies as many as possible in fast speed through direct investment to complement its R&D expenditure.

Market Age

Definition

The age of a market can be a tremendously important indicator for a company on how it should structure its new product development programs and marketing investments. Market age is defined as a time position of certain product in the product life cycle (PLC). The product life cycle is the indispensable measuring tool of the market age. PLC describes the sales pattern of a product over time. Generally, the time span begins with product introduction and ends with its obsolescence and replacement. While the form of the life cycle is fairly standard, it is subject to variations. The concept underlying the premise of product life cycle is that all products pass through the stages outlined below and illustrated in Chart 3.1

Chart 3.1 Market Age: Product Life Cycle (PLC) Stages

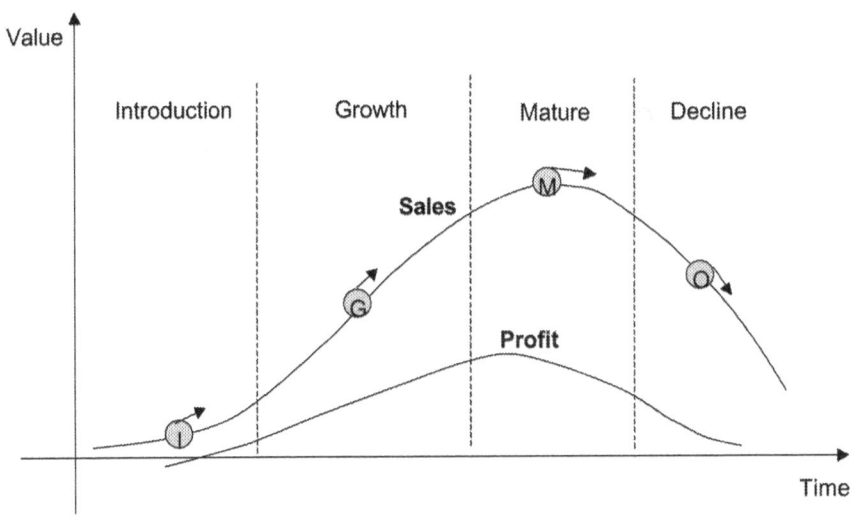

Any business is constantly seeking ways to grow future cash flows by maximizing revenue from the sale of products and services. Cash flow allows a company to maintain viability, invest in new product development and improve its workforce;

all in an effort to acquire additional market share and become a leader in its respective industry.

A consistent and sustainable cash flow (revenue) stream from product sales is key to any long term investment, and the best way to attain a stable revenue stream is a "Cash Cow" product, leading products that command a large market share in mature markets.

Also, market ages are becoming shorter and shorter and many products in mature industries are revitalized by product differentiation and market segmentation. Organizations increasingly reassess product life cycle cost and revenues as the time available to sell a product and recover the investment in it shrinks. Even as product life cycles shrink, the operating life of many products is lengthening. For example, the operating life of some durable goods, such as automobiles and appliances, has increased substantially. This leads the companies that produce these products to take their market age and service life into account when planning. Increasingly, companies are attempting to optimize market age revenue and profits through the consideration of product warranties, spare parts, and the ability to upgrade existing product. It's clear the concept of market age has a significant impact upon business strategy and performance. The product life cycle (PLC) identifies the distinct stages affecting sales of a product, from the product's inception until its retirement.

Basic Stages in the Product Life Cycle (PLC):

■ Introduction Stage
   The introduction stage represents a slow growth period. It is assumed that newly released products require some time to gain market acceptance, so sales in the initial period are slow.

   The firms in introduction stage seek to build product awareness and develop a market for the product.

■ Growth stage
   If the product introduction proved successful, rapid growth stages are reached and sales increase markedly. The firms in growth stage seek to build brand preference and increase market share.

■ Maturity stage

According to the concept of the life cycle, the market for any product is limited, and sales will generally fall short of their potential. When this point is reached, the market enters the maturation stage. If a product enters a market that has already moved into the mature stage, competition is intense because the product must compete for a share of an existing market that is not experiencing growth.

At maturity, the strong growth in sales diminishes. Competition may appear with similar products. The primary objective at this point is to defend market share while maximizing profit.

■ Decline stage

Once the market enters the decline stage, new products are not entering the market and demand levels are falling. At this point, the objective is to increase market share to maintain stable sales levels.

As sales decline, the firm has several options:

- Maintain the product, possibly rejuvenating it by adding new features and finding new uses.
- Harvest the product—reduce costs and continue to offer it, possibly to a loyal niche segment.
- Discontinue the product, liquidating remaining inventory or selling it to another firm and is willing to continue the product.

The life cycle goes further to assume that each product eventually is replaced by another or that initial rapid growth will end in decline.

The characteristics of each different stage can be understood by marketing mix shown in Figure 3.3.

Figure 3.3 Market Age: Product Life Cycle (PLC) Characteristics

Marketing Mix	Stage I Introduction	Stage II Growth	Stage III Maturity	Stage IV Decline
Product	Single	More	Full	Some
Price	Skimming/penetration	Gaining	Defending	Staying
Promotion	Informing/education	Diversification	Reminding	Minimal
Place (distribution)	Limited	More	Maximum	Fewer

Arguments on the market age in life cycle rise from some exceptions from common understanding. For instance, despite the rapidity of new product development and the pressure in some industries (e.g. the microcomputer industry) toward innovation, if a product or brand meets a need, it is not only hard to displace but can also enjoy a very long market age such as candy bar with longer than 25 years history.

The product life cycle (PLC) effect on product level is also argued in marketing research. From the advertisements in a 30 year-old magazine, it is duly noted that ice boxes have been replaced by refrigerators, black-and-white TVs have been replaced by color TVs, and 78 rpm record albums have been replaced by CDs. It also reveals that popular brands such as Kelvinator have disappeared, while the needs satisfied by the core products (e.g., refrigeration, entertainment) have continued. The product forms for satisfying those needs have changed, but the life cycles or benefits of the product class (product category) continue.

Chart 3.2 illustrates the relationship between product life cycle (PLC) and product level. Company with brand A has set a solid foothold in market. It has three strategic direction to expand its operation. The first method is to make great efforts to grab more market share from other brands; the second is to broaden product line and to create or enter into other product forms; the third method is to penetrate into other product class or categories. For some special cases, such as refrigeration equipment, the product class can enjoy a long life span and never fell. The retirement stage will never turn out.

Chart 3.2 Market Age: Product life cycle (PLC) in Product Level

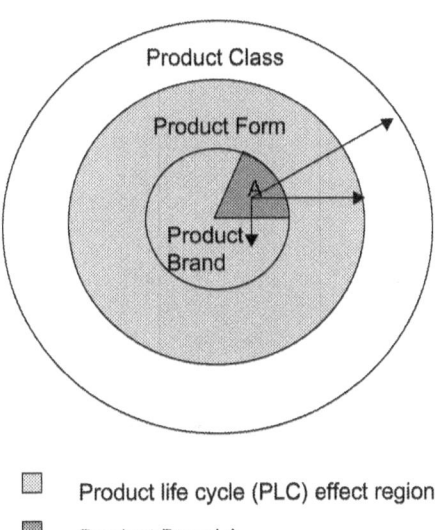

Product life cycle (PLC) effect region

Product Brand A

Therefore, the product life cycle (PLC) serves as little more than a framework for understanding managerial actions and is challenged to predict when the products/brands will move into another stage. The Product/Brand Life Cycle stages are dependent on marketing effort in light of situation-specific environmental constraints and just provide management with strategic direction but cannot be used in some exceptional fashions to determine a firm's activities and tactics.

Methods of Measurement

The concept of the product life cycle has become central to market forecasting. The stages of the life cycle form a framework used to analyze the dynamics and the primary factors that can impact a market segment and product sales.

The basic stages of the product life cycle can be expanded into a more-comprehensive model that better explains the various parts of the life of a product in the market. The list below outlines the various stages of the expanded product life cycle concept.

Stages of the Expanded Product Life Cycle are listed below and illustrated in Chart 3.3

1. Product R&D
2. Inception
3. Development
4. Exploitation
5. Maturation
6. Saturation
7. Descending
8. Obsolete

Chart 3.3 Market Age: Expanded Product Life Cycle

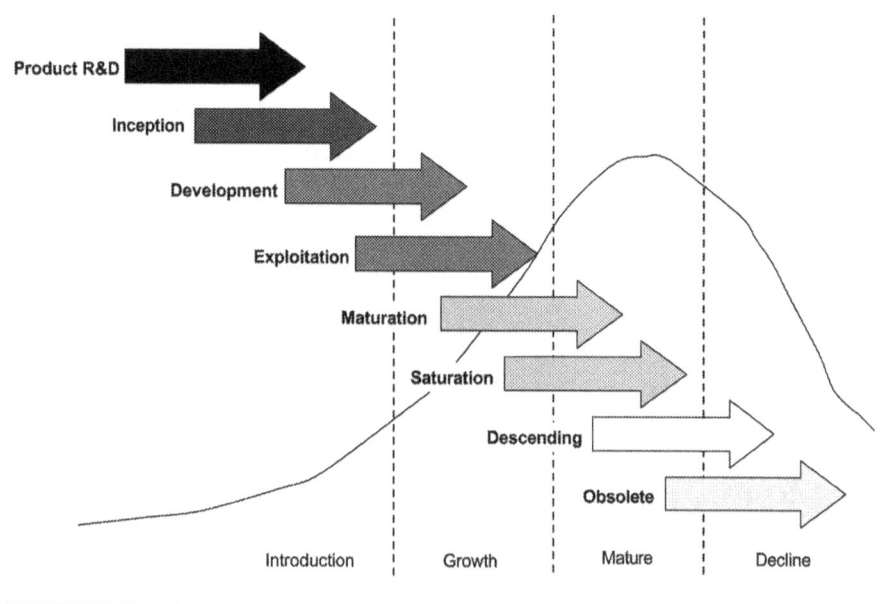

To calculate or measure market age, the following parameters need to be measured and monitored:

- Investment in R&D by year
- Number of competitors in the market by year
- Number of new entrants by year
- Number of competitors that left the market by year
- Market growth rate by year
- Market size by year
- Industry profitability by year
- A&P investment (such as advertising, trade shows, and direct sales forces) by year

The measurement of these parameters over time can determine what stage a given market is in. Figure 3.4 and Chart 3.4 below have provided details to make this determination:

Figure 3.4 Market Age: Measure the Stage of the Product Life Cycle

Stage	No. of Competitors	Market Growth (%)	Profits	Market Size	Investment
Product R&D	Unknown	None	None	0	Growing
Inception	Few	Highest	None	Small	High
Development	Growing Fast	High	Low	Samll	High
Exploitation	Moderate Growth	Good	Growing	Modest	High
Maturation	Stable	Low	High	Largest	Stable
Saturation	Stable	0	Lowering	Stable	Declining
Descending	Reducing	Negative	Moderate	Declining	Low
Obsolete	Few	Heavy Negative	Lowest	Small	Stopped

Chart 3.4 Market Age: Measure the Stage of the Product Life Cycle

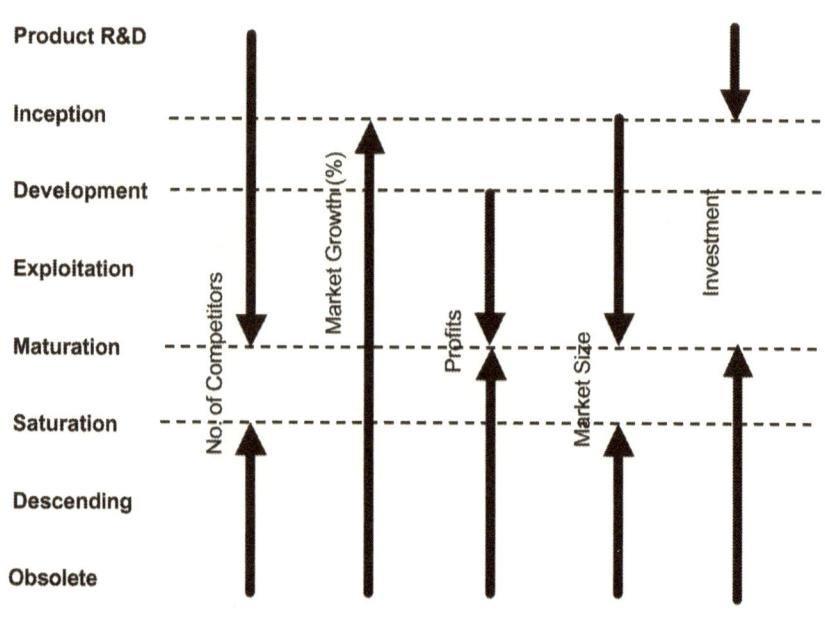

During the R&D stage, profits are nonexistent. In certain rare circumstances, profits are made early in the life cycle. However, generally profits are not made until the development of the market stage. It is usually at this point that products that have not reached profitability are withdrawn from the market.

Profits reach their zenith during the maturation stage; the saturation stages is characterized by steady to declining profits. The decline in profits typical during this stage is attributed to increased competition. Profits will continue to decline to the point where they no longer exist, and losses will take hold during the product decline stage and obsolete stage.

Thus, the life cycle is vital as a planning tool because the extent of profit changes during each stage of the life cycle. Forecasting and market planning over the medium term can be performed effectively using the product life cycle segments as the timing stages. The marketing strategies used will have to be modified as the product passes through each stage of the cycle.

Competition

Recognizing the current stage of the life cycle for a product type is vital to a firm considering the introduction of a product of that type. It is considerably easier to enter a market in a growth stage than it is to enter a saturated, mature market-place. Levels of competition in markets experiencing growth are considerably less intense than in mature markets where competitors are concerned about loss of sales and market share. Introducing a product into a market characterized by intense competition will probably prove expensive and result in retaliation from established competitors.

The product life cycle can be used to determine likely competitive trends. The list below outlines the typical levels of competition for each stage of the life cycle process:

- Product R&D

  New product R&D are conducted by some companies internally without market competition. Each company takes sneak research by itself and wants competitive intelligence about its rival at the same time.
- Introduction

  Levels of competition are practically non-existent since the company introducing the product can be the sole supplier.
- Development

  The market is still dominated by the product innovator, but other companies have entered the market and developed smaller shares.
- Exploitation

  A single company usually remains the primary force in the market although it may not be the product originator. The product innovator may have been overtaken by subsequent market entrants. In addition, the market leader may be fending off leadership challenges from other large competitors. Generally, the leading company's share will experience decline over this period as competitive activity in the market continues.
- Maturation

  The leading company usually still holds its leadership position, but its share is smaller than that of all other market competitors together.

■ Saturation

A host of smaller companies are all engaged in trying to secure a market niche they can dominate. Towards the conclusion of the saturation period, three of four competitors typically emerge to dominate the market. Vigorous marketing allows these competitors to hold the majority share.

■ Decline

The market leader during the saturation stage may be replaced by a competitor better suited to competing in small contracting markets. As specialized market segments continue to decline in scale, larger-scale producers cease to perceive them as profitable.

■ Obsolete

In obsolete stage, sales typically diminish across the board as products become more obsolete and are replaced by newer technology.

The primary reason for stressing the importance of the product life cycle is that for each stage or segment of the life cycle a different marketing strategy will prove best in meeting the unique demands of that stage of the life cycle.

Market factors such as demand and supply are changing constantly as they pertain to your company, market, and industry, so a detailed knowledge of the appropriate product life cycle can make your market strategy more timely and effective.

Case Study: Medical Ultrasound Technology

One electronic instrument giant in the medical ultrasound business had two products in the development phase in 1979: a real-time scanner and a B-scanner. The B-scanner project had started several years before, and at project commencement the second generation of its B-scan product was experiencing sales growth of 40 percent per year.

The technology for a B-scan image appeared to be in danger of being superseded by real-time images. B-scan images could be taken every 10 seconds, versus eight per second or more with the new real-time machines.

The B-scanning machines still offered some advantages in positioning, and the firm felt the image quality would be better with B-scanners, so the project continued. In 1980, the project came up for review. A careful analysis showed that the market for B-scan ultrasound equipment was indeed maturing. The unit and dollar sales for B-scanning instruments had stabilized in 1979-1981. The market, despite a slight recession at the time, was mature and had reached saturation. The real-time units were in a very rapid growth stage, expanding at over 300 percent per year. However, the real-time market was still a great deal smaller than the B-scan market, which was close to $100 million per year.

The big question was when the market would leave the maturity stage and move into the decline stage. This calculation would have to be based on market engineering, two separate investigations were taken:

- Interview competitors on their R&D plans for B-scanning equipment and their opinion of future technical trends
- Interview 1,000 medical practitioners to get a feel for their purchasing plans

During the competitive interviews 12 manufacturers were found having abandoned future R&D in the product area. This was extremely illuminating, as they were no longer supporting the product type in the trade press or at trade shows.

Customer interviews have confirmed the findings. Of the 675 responses received, fewer than 8 percent were interested in future purchases of B-scan equipment. Over 70 percent of survey respondents expressed strong interest in real-time imaging devices, and in the future would consider purchasing only these instruments.

It was now obvious that this product would be stillborn. The firm could never sell enough units to recoup initial R&D and product marketing investments. Unfortunately, the firm's management was composed largely of engineers who expressed disbelief in the results,

Eventually, the market was totally dead within 18 months. Six manufacturers went out of business, another cut prices by 75 percent. The remainder of the manufacturers had shifted to real-time instruments to cater to swings in market demand.

Unfortunately, our client not only lost the $5 million the firm allocated to R&D, but also an additional $3 million in marketing expenses.

The actual market history for this ultrasound market is presented in Figure 3.5 and Chart 3.5. It clearly illustrates the product life cycle of B-Scan images.

Figure 3.5 Market Age: Historical Growth of Ultrasound Market

Year	Unit Sales (B-Scan)	Growth Rate (%)	Unit Sales (Real Time)	Growth Rate (%)
1975	300	---	0	---
1976	500	66.7%	0	---
1977	700	40.0%	0	---
1978	900	28.6%	0	---
1979	1,100	22.2%	75	---
1980	1,150	4.5%	175	133.3%
1981	1,100	-4.3%	450	157.1%
1982	300	-72.7%	800	77.8%
1983	150	-50.0%	1,000	25.0%
1984	100	-33.3%	1,100	10.0%
1985	50	-50.0%	1,200	9.1%

Note: All figures are rounded.

Chart 3.5 Market Age: Historical Growth of Ultrasound Market

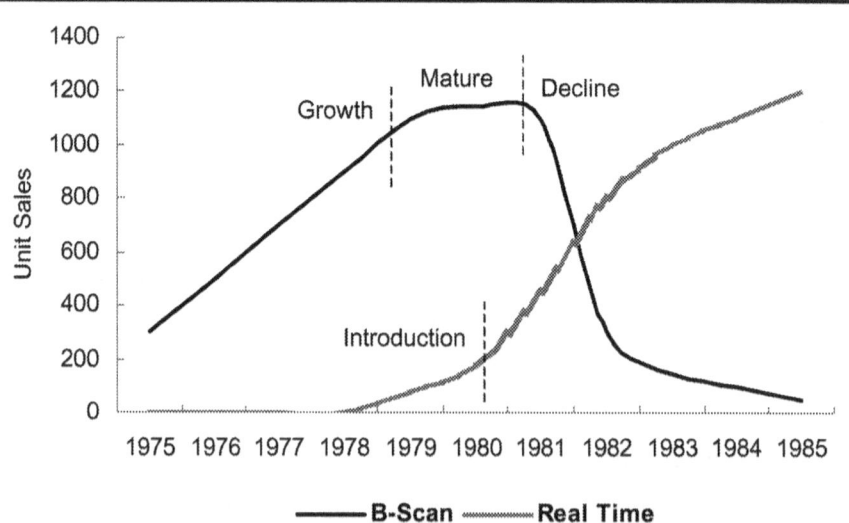

Note: All figures are rounded

Market Size

Definition

Market Size is a measurement evaluated by the total volume and or value of all sales in the market. Sales volume is measured in terms of the number of units of goods purchased, whilst sales value measures the total amount spent by customers on the volume of goods sold. Precise definition of the market size appears very important to marketers when determining market size.

Market size is one of the fundamental measurements that must be taken on the market. It is the standard measurement ruler against which all of a company's activities should be measured. For example, expenses for an R&D project should be related to market size. The same is true for sales force and marketing expenses. On one hand, CEO does not want to over-invest based on market size. On the other hand, CEO does not want to under-invest in large, fast-moving markets.

When a qualified marketing manager is informed by his analyst "The market for vacuum pumps is over $100 billion per year.", it will definitely leave lots of question marks in his head. Obviously, the essential premises of this market size are not stated clearly.

When monitoring or measuring a dynamic variable, the measurement must be well defined and all environmental premises considered. For example, the school administrators who face the competition with another school in the student enrollment want to know whether the parents' goal to maximize the children achievement has effect on enrollment. To document the student achievement level during enrollment, the market analysts need to note the status of various parameters such as:

- The educational concentration within a school district
- IQ measurement of student innate ability
- Teacher salary
- Class attendance rate
- College entry rate after graduation
- Pupil-teacher ratio

- Teacher union's bargain for local teachers
- ...etc.

It is obvious that fluctuations in these measurement variables could influence the student achievement dynamics. For the same reason, when the analyst confidently states that the market for vacuum pumps is $100 billion, it should be requested that all documentation on how this measurement was taken and the status of all relevant parameters to gauge the impacts on the forecast should be presented.

"MUST DO" principle illustrated in Chart 3.6 and Figure 3.6 is a preliminary knowledge base for market size measurement which is a useful reminder to marketers to take circumstance variables into consideration and has been well accepted by many market research companies

Chart 3.6 Market Size: "MUST DO" Principle

Figure 3.6 Market Size: "MUST DO" Principle

Variables	Example
Method	Secondary data sources
	Competitor interviews
	End-user surveys
	In-house database
	Experience
Unit	Currency
	Units
	Volume
Scope	Product:
	Submersible pumps
	Circulator pumps
	Sealless pumps
	Turbine pumps
	Customer:
	Female
	Annual salary over $100,000
	Age above 60
	Region:
	World
	U.S.
	EU/Japan
Time	One year (usually assumed)
	Six months
	One month
Date	1987
	1999
	2004
Observation	Production
	Consumption

Method

The common method adopted to measure market size is to combine secondary and primary research together. Some valued figures can be found in statistics publication or released news/articles on internet which can provide market researchers indicative data to help work out the more precise market size. Nevertheless, statistics data are not always correct and varies with different survey scope. Cross-check by interviews is necessary and probably a must to ensure reliability of obtained data.

Unit

Unit is determined by the measuring base of market size: volume or value. Normally, volume based market size is required for natural resource and raw material market, value based market size is more required by FMCG, both volume based and value based market sizes are required for industrial products.

Scope

Scope is a very important factor not just for market size but for entire research project. It can be classified into three categories: product, customer, and region. Product scope must be identified for market size. Some product definition is ambiguous to market researchers. For example, "3C" product is an inexplicable definition to anyone. It is not clarified how many types of products it contains. It is necessary to specify the product before starting research. Customer scope is special for some products having certain customer group, such as sanitary napkin. Region scope is a palpable geographic research base for survey.

Time

Time period is a time characteristics of market size describing the validation of obtained market size. It must be clearly stated in the market size chart.

Date

The production date of obtained market size must be available for later check which can facilitate marketing manager or analysts to track the historic market size.

Observation

It is pitiful to ignore the observation perspective in market size research since from various penetration perspectives can generate different result. Take plastic coating as example. The figure of market size turns out to be quite different if the data is generated from production perspective or consumption perspective since the wastage in coating spraying is not inclusive.

Methods of Measurement

The importance of making accurate measurements of market size should not exaggerated. Virtually, accurate report on market size can help company decide on its target sales revenue, potential investment, and allocation of efficient resources.

Relatively simple analysis which builds on data is readily available in most companies. All companies make a rough estimate of that parameter based on in-house sales data. Some of the larger companies in broader product segments have a dedicated market research staff that accurately tracks the size of various market segments within market segments of the particular industry. However, less-significant product segments that the research community tends to ignore must rely on experienced salesperson or on government statistics.

An intern marketing manager assistant has been asked to size the market for a specific service in his country, he don't have any information about how many companies exist in this market, and how many of them are large, medium or small. He has no idea of calculating a sample size to carry out the survey and how to conduct a good estimation.

There are many methods by which market size can be calculated. These methods can be categorized into following groups:

■ Extrapolation from sample

This approach is usually employed to analyze the FMCG market. General speaking, it is to take a random sample from the customer population to see what percentage of the sample use the product.

The sample size is based on the size of the user population and the degree of accuracy needed, in other words, it depends on how detailed the required information is. A statistician may calculate the number of responses required to give a statistically valid reading if the total number of companies in this market is available.

A pilot survey among 25-50 companies is necessary when deciding the sample size. If the responses of pilot survey are overwhelmingly similar, a larger study may not be required to waste time and money.

Whereas, normally, if the responses from all companies are weighted equally, probably only 100-200 responses are needed. If the result is weighted based on company size, 150 responses probably needed from each size category. Likewise, if the response by industry required, a representative sample from each relevant industry needs to be taken.

This method still has pitfall. If there are few end-users, this is an accurate measurement. However, as the end-user base increases, the cost rises and the accuracy of the measurement falls. A smaller sample will have to be taken and extrapolated to approximate the entire user population. Whereas, a sample of 1,000 companies does not give a guarantee that it still represents the universe in a systematic way; the results could still show biased indication.

■ Government statistics
A shortcut to get the data of market size is to search on the internet to find the government statistics. Sometimes the marketers come across a problem the government figure is far different from the realistic market size. Why? Government collects data on new companies but fail to update the databases when a company stops to operate. The smaller the company, the worse the discrepancy is. The government statistics only can play as indicative role. All data needs to be verified by primary research.

■ Estimates from interviews
This approach is always a helpful method to market opportunity analysis as well as determination of market size which is used most often by research firms, is based on a series of competitive interviews where each competitor is asked for an estimate of the market size. These estimates are sometimes weighted and then averaged for the market size calculation. To visit the market involved to talk to people who might actually know the answers to the market size will not take more than a few days to find the answer.

- Estimates on potential

When decision markers want to know the potential market, it is feasible to adopt this approach. To determine a particular potential market, one recommended original research one-on-one interviews is not only talking to potential customers but also involving native researchers if possible and including expert opinion polls about the market size and potential growth rate. These experts may be companies own sales managers, outside consultants, top executives and government officials that must on occasion talk, comment directly use about the particular regional market or talk directly to potential customers. The key is to use the information to forecast demand through triangulation—comparing estimates produced through different sources.

- Determination on production

Some marketers estimate the market size based on the current rates of production or production capacity. But production is also a poor indication of customer demand because production and actual sales are rarely perfectly coordinated.

Bottom-up Method

Bottom up approach refers to a building style that starts the selection process with an examination of individual companies, followed by a forecast of industry prospects and general economic conditions. This is in contrast to top down approach, which starts with a forecast of general economic conditions, followed by the identification of those industry sectors thorough to individual company.

Particularized into marketing research, bottom-up method is defined as the process of quantifying any market by aggregating the most logical constituent elements of that market. The bottom-up approach is far more time-consuming but is more accurate. In essence, it uses a series of interviews with all suppliers to determine quantities sold by each company in the period. These are added together to give the total market size.

The typical process and model followed by numerous market researchers are illustrated in Chart 3.7 and Figure 3.7

Chart 3.7 Market Size: Typical Bottom-up Process

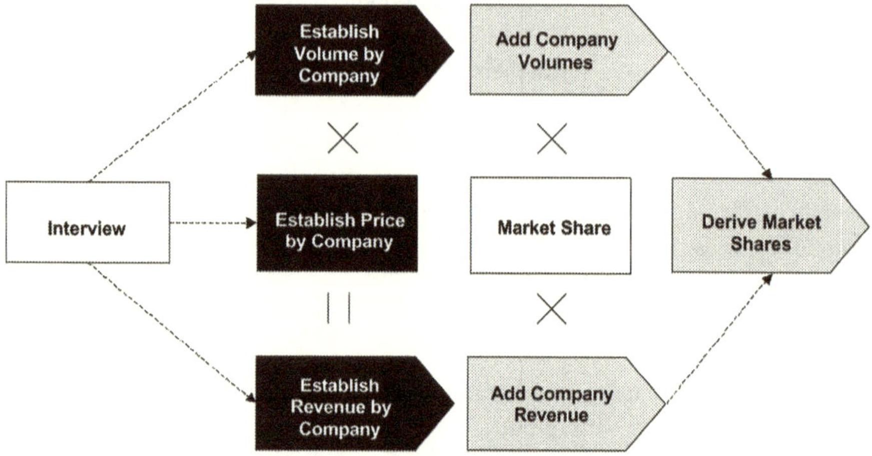

Figure 3.7 Market Size: Bottom-up Model

	Method A			Method B		Method C
	Revenue	Volume		Price	Revenue	Market Size =
Company A	$AA mil	aa mil	x	$ A	= $AA mil	Revenue(Company A,B,C,…)
Company B	$BB mil	bb mil	x	$ B	= $BB mil	x
Company C	$CC mil	cc mil	x	$ C	= $CC mil	M/S%(Company A,B,C,…)
Others	$ OO mil	oo mil	x	$ O	= $OO mil	
…	…	…		…	…	
Total (Market Size)	$ XX mil (by value)	xx mil (by volume)	x	$ X	= $XX mil (by value)	

Note: M/S refers to market share.

The bottom-up process varies by market scenario. Appropriate adaptation to different marketing circumstance needs to be taken to achieve more accurate market size.

■   80/20 market

This market has high market concentration, so bottom-up can be reasonable approach to be employed to calculate the market size since bottom-up revenues for 20% of the companies can account for 80% market. The total market size can be easily derived by market share divided by 0.8. But the primary premise to use bottom-up method is to confirm with the revenue of top 20% companies with their market share. Empirically, this process typically applies to mature markets with high barriers to entry, such as machine tool markets, telecom long distance services market, diagnostic imaging equipment market.

■   Fragmented market

This market has very low market concentration. Each competitor has minor market share. The following tiered approach is suggested for better estimate of the market size.

Tier 1: Bottom-up

Tier 2: R x N

Tier 3: R x N

Where R is average revenue of companies in tier 2 (tier 3), N is the number of companies in Tier 2 (Tier 3). This process typically applies to markets with low barriers to entry, such as process control software market, packaging machinery market.

■   Emerging market

Emerging market is a new born market with few not easily identifiable players. Unpredictable new entrants generate more difficulties to market sizes determination. It even does not have historical basis for market size estimate.

Two groups of players, both current and emerging players, need to be identified. Market researchers should focus more on market opportunity than on market size. Market opportunity can be defined by demand-side bottom-up model with identification of OEM/End-User markets and potential demand for new emerging products in each OEM/End-user market, such as genomics, IP telephony, smart cards, etc.

■   Markets with product/service mix

This type of market is a mixture of product and service such as test & measure-ment, product sales, rental/leasing, telemetry etc. The important principle to determine the market size of such market is to bear explicit market separation through the project. It is painful to ignore the importance of market definition in calculation. First, identify which company offers both product and service and which company offers only one or the other. Then, split the revenue of each com-pany by product vs. service. The service revenues typically accounted for accrual basis.

Case Study: Chinese Tractors Market

A 50-year-old tractor manufacturing company want to tap into China. But it knows nothing about Chinese tractor market. Strategic planning department is incumbent to identify the opportunities for the company. Their primary job is to understand the market.

Tractor market has myriads of products which is a big barriers to the estimate of market size. The marketing department has collected relevant data of major com-petitors in Chinese market. The problem facing to them is how to conduct data analysis.

Secondary research reflects that Chinese tractor market is a type of 80/20 market with relatively high concentration. The number of dominant players is over 15, still subject validate. Further, the different secondary resource shows different figure which brings divergence in figuring out market size.

The strategic planning department decided to utilize bottom-up method. The first step is to establish effective revenue database. Method B in Figure 3.7 was employed to calculate the company revenue. The reason to use Method B is that the machinery product is easily countable goods the unit of which is commonly accepted in statistics. Furthermore, price is not sensitive topic in interview with competitor. The respondents may answer such question without any contempla-tion; they may think you are a big potential customer and fax you the product quotation within one minute. Nevertheless, it can be difficult to catch the exact company revenues within short conversation if Method A is used. It is even hard to get it through face to face interviews since it is the company confidential every-one knows that.

The company commissioned the external research company to conduct interviews to get the essential data of volume and price. The database was established by interviewee's inputs. A detailed price list was developed by company for each specific model. A problem comes up with the price analysis—how to achieve the average price by company. A simple and cursory way to handle this is to average all specific price. This leaves a remarkable deviation from precise since the sales volume for each specific model is different. More accurate and complex method is to assign the weight to the price in calculation.

Whereas, actually to get the exact sales volume for each specific model is not feasible in market research since no respondent is willing to share such information with callers. He even will hesitate to give it to the counterparts. The interviewers have to try another way to ask about the product ration. The product ratio means the percentage of specific group of products accounts for. Thus the average price can be calculated by aggregating the figures from the average price of specific product segment multiplying product ration. The detailed analysis process is explained in Chart 3.8.

Then after that, a quick market engineering overview of the company was conducted by strategic planning department to determine where to position itself in the market. Three distinct overviews was developed on three different product segment.

The first and perhaps the most important parameter to be determined was the firm's size in each segmented market in which its product segment competed. Of course, knowing the market size and volume of sales of each of the product segment, market share can be easily calculated immediately, as shown in Figure 3.8:

Chart 3.8 Market Size: Data Analysis Process

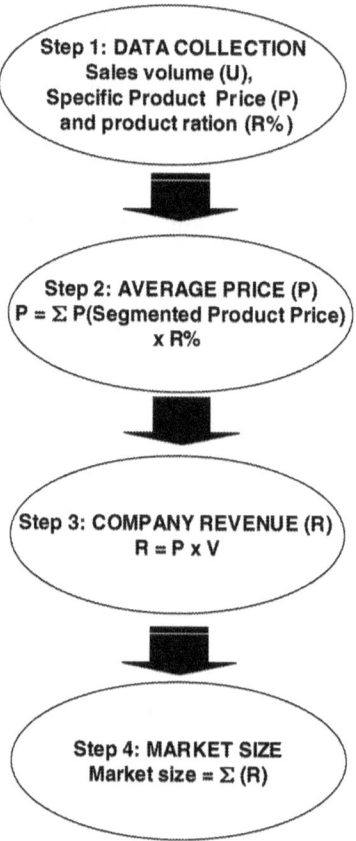

Figure 3.8 Market Size: Market Share Calculations

Division	Sales ($ Million)	Market Size ($ Million)	Market Share (%)
Light Duty (>25hp)	80	850	9.4
Medium Duty (25≤x≤50hp	54	65	83.0
Heavy Duty (<50hp)	39	90	43.3

Note: All figures are rounded.

This certainly was an eye-opener. It immediately showed management panel that the firm was looking for greener pastures while completely overlooking the green grass in its own backyard. It was quite obvious that the growth opportunity would most likely be found in the light duty (>25hp) segment.

This analysis brought marketing manager to the conclusion that if the company had as many salespeople per market size in the light duty (>25hp) tractor market as it did in other segments; there would be dozens of times as many salespeople to address that market. Moreover, R&D spending would be increased by hundreds of million as well, if it were in proportion to other segments.

Strategic recommendations

- Company must stop its investigations into acquisitions and product development outside its areas of expertise.
- Company should increase the number of salespeople in the light duty (>25hp) tractor segment and the sales force. In the mean time, company should observe the level of sales per salesperson to determine if they remained stable.
- The firm should allocate additional funds for product development to grow the light duty (>25hp) tractor in line with the two other segments the company addressed.

Market Growth Rate

Definition

Growth rates can be defined as the rate of increase in size per unit time. The size can be gauged by revenue or unit shipment. Unit time generally is one year in marketing research. The growth rate in marketing research includes individual growth rate of specific company and market growth rate of overall market either of which is a key indicator of the health of company or growth trend of positioned market. As an aircraft pilot analogy, growth rates can be likened to a tail wind. The tail wind can create a large difference between ground speed and air speed. If the pilot were to use air speed alone he would miss his destination. Assume the revenues of one toy company are growing at 15 percent per year. Superficially, this appears impressive. If, however, market revenues are expanding at an average of 25 percent per annum, the company absolutely has a serious problem. Relative to the "speed" of the overall market, the company is missing out on the benefit of some "tail wind" that its competitors are enjoying.

The growth rate concept is simple enough on the surface. However, it is extremely important to remain aware of the specifics underlying the measurement. Some typical market parameters are described below:

- Product segments
- Time period
- Geographic areas
- Measurement units
- Customer segments

Knowledge of market growth is essential to the market engineer. Market growth is a key indicator of the health of company. If the company sales growth is greater than or equal to market growth, the firm is comparatively healthy. If, however, the company's growth in sales is less than market growth, it is very likely the firm is in competitive trouble.

The market growth rate is also a key indication of the product's stage in the product life cycle. A high growth rate will usually indicate the market is in the growth phase, where growth is high and saturation is low. A lower, more-stable growth rate indicates product maturation and, of course, a negative market growth rate indicates the product decline stage. Company will want to alter its market strategy for each of the stages of the product life cycle.

Compound annual growth rate (CAGR)

Pick up any financial magazine or business newspaper and term compounded annual growth rate (CAGR) always comes into your eyes. CAGR is a way for a company to express their rate of growth over a number of years to the public, investors, and internally which is defined as the year over year growth rate of an investment over a specific period of time calculated by taking the *n*th root of the total percentage growth rate where *n* is the number of years in the period being considered. It can be written as:

$$CAGR = \left(\frac{E}{B}\right)^{\left(\frac{1}{N}\right)} - 1$$

Where E = ending value
     B = beginning value
     N = No. of years

In the financial arena, companies generally apply this formula to a base amount that they feel is an important component of their operations. Probably the most common component used in business is revenue (i.e., sales). However, this formula can be applied to several other parts of a business operation such as marketing research. CAGR can play as an imaginary marketing indicator that describes the market/company growth rate at which the market/company grew as though it had grown at a steady rate which indicates to the company what the market size or company revenue will really be at the end of the forecast period.

CAGR has two characteristics as follows:

- *Imaginary.* It doesn't represent reality. It is an expected figure extrapolated from historical growth and delineates the future growth in the forecast period.

- *Smooth.* There ought to be a deviation between actual growth and CAGR "smooth" growth. Obviously, CAGR doesn't reflect the market volatility at certain time point.

Methods of Measurement

The measurement of market growth is quite simple if you are dealing with a market that you have been tracking regularly over a period of years. This is rarely the case. The great majority of companies have not been taking regular measurements of market size, so calculation becomes more difficult.

There are many ways to calculate the growth of a market or product segment. The use of secondary sources is the easiest and least expensive way to get an estimate of market growth rates. Many market engineering companies publish information of this nature.

Two problems may be encountered with published information. First, unless the company is a participant in a multi billion dollar industry such as portable computer manufacturing, the chances are the empirical information required to quantify this market does not exist. Nine out of ten times, the accurate statistics for specific product segments do not exist. Second, the overwhelming majority of information referencing the size of various markets and growth rates is poorly documented and inaccurate. The data gleaned from magazines, newspapers, or government sources should not be used unless the methodology used in gathering the information is verified. Magazines and newspapers will often quote sources without taking the time to verify the information being supplied to them. As for government statistics such as Commerce Department statistics of US, the statistics are compiled in a cursory way that a general survey was mailed out to manufacturers in the industry. Of the 200 surveys mailed out, a 5 to 10 percent response is claimed. From this the published results are extrapolated.

The problems with these agencies intensified when they are questioned about which piece of equipment is included in which product category. Different types of equipment are grouped together without the slightest understanding of the equipment's applications. Also, the surveys used were incomprehensible regarding specific product categories.

On the contrary, many private market engineering organizations are more than willing to describe their data gathering methodologies in-depth, and provide detailed descriptions of their product segment breakdowns. Primary research such as telephone interviews of industry participants is used by market analysts to gather information for use in computing growth rates. They learn to interpret the quantitative and qualitative information received in an interview and to formulate growth rates based on that information.

To measure market growth rates accurately, the effect of each individual company growth needs to be taken into consideration so that each of the competitor's growth rates must be weighted by its market share. The weighted growth rate can be expressed in the following formulation:

$$WG = G \times M/S$$

Where **WG** = weighted growth rate
     G = company growth rate
     M/S = market share

Then the overall market growth rate can be calculated as follows:

$$MG = \sum WG$$

Where **MG** = market growth rate.

This becomes extremely important if one or two of the market participants have a dominant market share. Their performance will need to have a higher weight and more significant contribution to market growth

The best information can be used to calculate market growth would be unit and dollar sales for the preceding years. Two suggested methods of gathering this information are as follows:

■ End-user surveys
■ Competitive interviews and analyses

Comparing these two approaches, the end-user survey is more expensive and time consuming because it requires a large sample size; the competitive interview and analysis method which is widely accepted is more effective but more difficult in collecting data. For competitive analysis method, by carefully examining competitor's growth rates over a period of years, researchers can get a firm idea of overall market growth. Although the accuracy of the method is far from precise, generally within 8 percent to 10 percent, the obtained information is extremely informative.

The problem with doing the market research is that it is often difficult to get the information from other manufacturers. However, by making good use of readily available annual reports, quarterly reports, and by interviewing marketing managers, salespeople, and other executives, a pretty good impression of market growth rates can be put together.

Market Growth Forecast Model

Market growth forecast model is a time series forecast closely analyzing the changes in the variables such as commodity unit, dollar sales, and growth rate with time period. Such projection of trend is among the most widely used forecasting methods for market research. Provided researchers can separate the dependent from the independent variables and observe how these independent variables have behaved in the past and project them forward into subsequent periods.

The advocated methodology of this model shown in Chart 3.9 for market researchers to follow when formulating a market trend projection is outlined below. It is quite simple and very helpful to build a credible basis for a market or sales forecast. This basis can assist marketers in carrying out more accurate trend projection.

- Step I: Measure historical trends
    - Conduct secondary research from accumulate published information, industry reports, and so on.
    - Conduct primary research with leading market competitors.
    - The required historical trend information should include price trends, historical sales, market shares and so forth.

- Step II: Determine the base year data
    - Conduct interviews with the following groups in order to determine the accuracy of the base year numbers and the projecting trends:
    Producers
    Government agencies
    End users
    Market research experts

- Step III: Analyze market drivers and restraints
    - Identify market drivers and restraints based on profuse secondary research and primary research.
    - Identify the impact scales to market growth of all drivers/restraints such as low, medium, and high.
    - Determine the time scale such as short term, medium term and long term for each driver/restraint.

- Step IV: Weight drivers/restraints
    - Determine the weights for all drivers/restraints

- Step V: Generate future data
    - Calculate the data within forecast period.

- Step VI: Calculate compound annual growth rate (CAGR)
    - Determine the market growth indicator

Chart 3.9 Growth Rate: Market Growth Rate Forecast Model

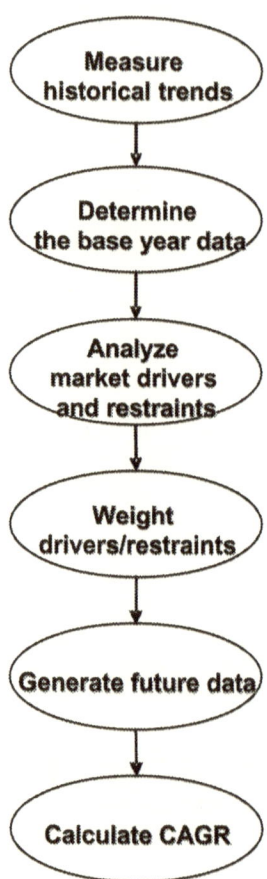

Case Study: Standard Products Market in China

A world leading standard products manufacturer wants to set up a market penetration project on China since the company recognized the need for a comprehensive focused strategy for expanding its presence in China due to the large size of the China market and anticipated long-term rapid growth.

To develop a actionable marketing strategy, the first step is to identify the general market which can provide decision makers a broad picture of total market including market challenges, drivers and restraints, market size, market share and growth forecast etc.

During a ten-year period, this company did not project market growth. The firm's management operated under the assumption that since their product had helped create the market, market growth would be similar to their own sales growth. This assumption leads to erroneous impression on the future market.

A systematic market growth forecast model was employed to generate a insightful market trend projection to calibrate the market focus and help develop correct marketing strategy.

The historical revenues of major industrial participants were collected from primary interviews with competitors and experts in the standard products industry. Bottom-up method was used to calculate the historical market size. Then the calculated data as shown in Figure 3.9 were compared with secondary sources to ensure the accuracy and reliability.

Figure 3.9 Growth Rate: Historical market size

Year	Market Size ($ Million)
2001	373.0
2002	496.5
2003	607.3
2004	708.1
CAGR	23.8%

Note: All figures are rounded.

The base year figure was determined at $708.1 million in 2004 which is a basis for future projection. The compound annual growth rate was calculated and valued at 23.8%.

Chart 3.10 Growth rate: Time scale of driver/restraint

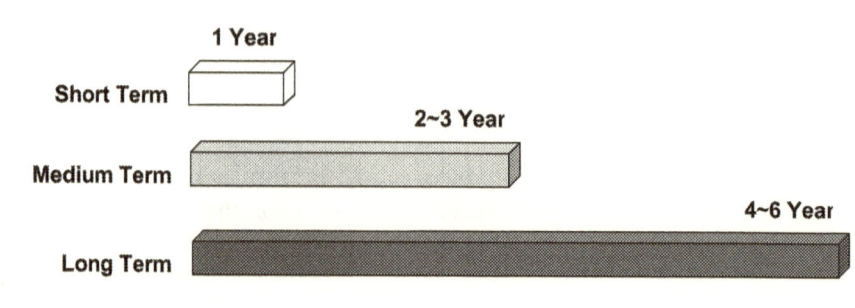

Market drivers and restraints were identified by macroeconomic environmental analysis such as PESTE and STEEP. The time scale for each driver/restraint was defined as short term, medium term and long term in Chart 3.10. The impact scale was also determined as shown in Figure 3.10

Figure 3.10 Growth rate: Impact scale of driver/restraint

Impact Scale	Index
No impact	1.00
Very low	1.10
Low	1.20
Low/Med	1.30
Medium	1.40
Med/High	1.50
High	1.60
Very high	1.70

Note: All figures are rounded.

Figure 3.11 Growth rate: Weight and index drivers and restraints

	2004 (Base year)	2005 (1 year)	2006 (2 year)	2007 (3 year)	2008 (4 year)	2009 (5 year)	2010 (6 year)
Driver 1	-	$S_{d1} \times I1_{d1}$	$M_{d1} \times I2d_1$	$M_{d1} \times I3_{d1}$	$L_{d1} \times I4_{d1}$	$L_{d1} \times I5_{d1}$	$L_{d1} \times I6_{d1}$
Driver 2	-	$S_{d2} \times I1_{d2}$	$M_{d2} \times I2_{d2}$	$M_{d2} \times I3_{d2}$	$L_{d2} \times I4_{d2}$	$L_{d2} \times I5_{d2}$	$L_{d2} \times I6_{d2}$
Driver 3	-	$S_{d3} \times I1_{d3}$	$M_{d3} \times I2_{d3}$	$M_{d3} \times I3_{d3}$	$L_{d3} \times I4_{d3}$	$L_{d3} \times I5_{d3}$	$L_{d3} \times I6_{d3}$
...	...	...	...	...	...	...	...
Restraint 1	-	$S_{r1} \times I1_{r1}$	$M_{r1} \times I2_{r1}$	$M_{r1} \times I3_{r1}$	$L_{r1} \times I4_{r1}$	$L_{r1} \times I5_{r1}$	$L_{r1} \times I6_{r1}$
Restraint 2	-	$S_{r2} \times I1_{r2}$	$M_{r2} \times I2_{r2}$	$Mr_2 \times I3r_2$	$Lr_2 \times I4r_2$	$L_{r2} \times I5_{r2}$	$L_{r2} \times I6_{r2}$
Restraint 3	-	$S_{r3} \times I1_{r3}$	$M_{r3} \times I2_{r3}$	$M_{r3} \times I3_{r3}$	$L_{r3} \times I4_{r3}$	$L_{r3} \times I5_{r3}$	$L_{r3} \times I6_{r3}$
...	...	...	...	...	...		

S_{di}, M_{di}, L_{di} = weight for driver i (di) to short term, medium term, long term scale
S_{ri}, M_{ri}, L_{ri} = weight for restraint i (ri) to short term, medium term, long term scale
Ij_{di}/ Ij_{ri} = impact index number for driver i (di)/restraint i (ri)

Both drivers and restraints were weighted and indexed as shown in Figure 3.11. There are underlying principles need to comply with:

$$\sum (S, M, L)_{di} + \sum (S, M, L)_{ri} = 100\%$$

$$Ij_{di} = \frac{1}{Ij_{ri}}$$

Where $(S,M,L)_{di}$ = any of S_{di}, M_{di}, L_{di}
$(S,M,L)_{ri}$ = any of S_{ri}, M_{ri}, L_{ri}

The forecast market size as shown in Chart 3.11 was calculated by following formulas:

$$MS = MS_p \times \left\{ \sum \left[(S, M, L)_{di} \times Ij_{di} \right] + \sum \left[(S, M, L)_{ri} + Ij_{ri} \right] \right\}$$

Where MS_p = market size of previous year
$(S,M,L)_{di}$ = any of S_{di}, M_{di}, L_{di}
$(S,M,L)_{ri}$ = any of S_{ri}, M_{ri}, L_{ri}

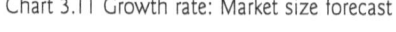

Chart 3.11 Growth rate: Market size forecast

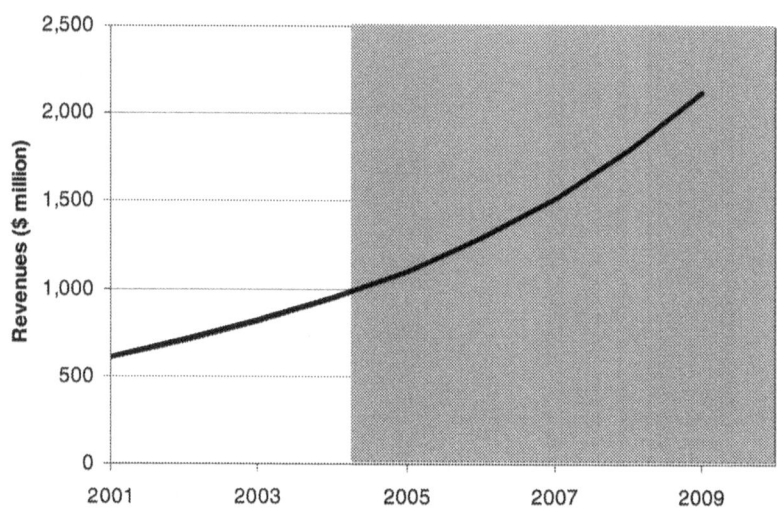

Note: All figures are rounded.

Strategic recommendations:

Today, the company has its own internal market engineering staff that continuously monitors competitors' sales. With these figures, they are able to calculate with relative accuracy the annual growth of the market, total market size, and market share.

This system has made the company a great deal more marketing-oriented in its competitive responses and levels of investment in the company's marketing department. Unfortunately, it is extremely difficult to regain lost market share in a mature market.

Market Share

Definition

Sales figures do not necessarily indicate how a firm is performing relative to its competitors. Rather, changes in sales simply may reflect changes in the market size or changes in economic conditions.

Market share is among the most vital parameters in the market monitoring process. Like temperature to human health, market share is a key indicator of the health of company. The majority of companies overestimate their market shares mostly because they do not engage in comprehensive competitor monitoring. Marketing managers are often excessively optimistic when estimating market share. Rarely is the market share parameter underestimated.

One of the most important aspects of market share to monitor is how it changes over time. Watching market share over time should be a vital part of strategic marketing plan.

Market share also suggests the safety and stability of firm's position in the market. A very small market share, less than 10 percent, could possibly be absorbed by a large competitor, while a 50 percent market share is far more difficult to be lost.

Therefore, every firm must be concerned about its share of the markets and market segments in which it competes. The firm's performance relative to competitors can be measured by the proportion of the market that the firm is able to capture. This proportion is referred to as the firm's market share and is the percentage of market unit volume or dollar value held by a company as a proportion of total market size.

Market share is merely the proportion of total market or industry sales made by one of the competing companies. Market share may be determined either on a value basis (sales price multiplied by volume) or on a unit basis (number of units shipped or number of customers served):

$$M/S = \frac{F}{S}$$

Where M/S = market share, F = firm's sales (volume/revenue), S = total market sales (volume/revenue).

While the firm's own sales figures are readily available, total market sales are more difficult to determine. Usually, this information is available from trade associations and market research firms.

The difference between market share by value and market share by volume indicates the price gap between specific price and average market price. The mathematic relation is formulated as follows:

$$\Delta M/S_{(Value-Volume)} = M/S_{(Value)} - M/S_{(Volume)}$$

$$= \frac{R}{S_r} - \frac{V}{S_v}$$

$$= \frac{R \times P_i}{S_v \times P} - \frac{V}{S_v}$$

$$= \frac{R \times P_i}{S_v \times P} - \frac{V \times P}{S_v \times P}$$

$$= \frac{V \times (P_i - P)}{S_v \times P}$$

Where M/S = market share, R = revenue, V = volume, S_r = market size by value, S_v = market size by volume, P_i = specific price, P = average market price

If $\Delta M/S_{(value-volume)} < 0$, namely $P_i - P < 0$, that means the product price is lower than the average market price. If $\Delta M/S_{(value-volume)} = 0$, namely $P_i - P = 0$, that means the product price is equal to the average market price. If $\Delta M/S_{(value-volume)} > 0$, namely $P_i - P > 0$, that means the product price is higher than the average market price.

The difference between the market share of a particular business and that of its competitors depends on the combination of differences in quality and characteristics of their respective product, in the price, the distribution system and channels, the advertising and the promotion of sales (marketing mix) [3~5].

$$M/S = f\{Q,P,D,A,P\}$$

Where M/S = market share, Q = product quality and characteristics, P = price, D = capacity and efficiency of distribution system, A = capacity and efficiency of advertising system, P = capacity and efficiency of promotion system

Of course, depending on the market conditions and the forms of competition, each one of these variables takes on special significance. For example, whereas in the Fast Manufacturing Consumer Goods (FMCG) industry, good distribution and effective advertising constitute every important variables for the conquest of the market share, in the telecommunication industry or human interface interaction industry, these variables are only of secondary important, the primary role being played by the product's price and technical advantages.

In general, attaining the highest market share is a desirable objective. The rule is that, regardless of the price of your product, you will remain more profitable than your competitors if you have higher market share. However, you must be careful to ensure that your market is clearly defined. The underlying reason why small companies can function profitably in large marketplaces is that they have actually developed a large share of a small segment of the total market.

Nevertheless, there is exception for some unique low share companies who are very successful in achieving profitability. Their success is mainly due to certain features of strategy that contribute a lot to their profitabilities [1]:

- Careful segmentation of existing and potential markets
- Efficient use of research and development funds
- Be small
- Pervasive chief executive's influence.

Market share is strongly associated with profitability and thus many firms seek to increase their sales relative to competitors. The relationship between market share and profitability was determined on the following three basic 'intervening' variables [2]:

- *Economies of scale and experience effects.* These phenomena which are determined exclusively by the size of the market share result in the reduction of the cost of production and distribution. Higher volume can be instrumental in developing a cost advantage.
- *Market power.* The greater the market of an enterprise, the greater the market power it has. This market share allows it to 'bargain more effectively, to "administer" prices and in the end, to realize significantly higher prices for a particular product.' Market leaders have an advantage in negotiations with suppliers and channel members and have clout that they can use reputation to their advantage.
- *Quality of management.* 'Good managers, including perhaps lucky ones are successful in achieving high shares of their prospective markets; they are also skillful in controlling costs, in getting the maximum productivity from their employees and so on.'

Methods of Measurement

An accurate measurement of market share is dependent on several factors:

- The *satisfaction* of market definition. This would clarify the confusion such as which products to include, which geographical region to cover, which demographic customer group to interview etc.
- The *availability* of reliable and up-to-date information. Whether the secondary data source is authoritative and precise to report the market.
- The *feasibility* of adopted measurement methods. For example, secondary research, primary research, data verification etc.
- The *relevance* of measures of share. For example, should market share be calculated in terms of sales revenues, profits, produced volume or some other measures that marketers generally recognized as valid?

As to the measurement methods, starting from the preliminary secondary research may create a valuable database for further analysis. It is a instrumental approach to general broadly defined industrial products such as tractor, painting, TV set, not for specific products such as light duty tractor, polyurethane wood coating, LCD TV set.

Some useful secondary research sources are listed as follows:

- One-stop-shopping for market share
  Ex: Business rankings annual, Market share reporter, Consumer USA, U.S. Market trends and forecasts etc.

- Researching newspaper/journal article about market share: databases
  Ex: ABI Information Global, Canadian Newsstand

- Analysts' reports
  Ex: Dominion Bond Rating Service

- Company annual reports
  Ex: Mergent Online

- Industry surveys
  Ex: NetAdvantage

- Lists, rankings
  Ex: Encyclopedia of American industries, manufacturing and distribution USA, Ward's business directory of U.S. private and public companies.

Followed by primary research, two primary groups can be targeted to interview or survey to make the market share measurement which generates two analyzing perspectives:
- Competitors analysis
- End-users analysis

Competitors analysis

In practice, the most reliable, accurate, and fast approach is to base market share measurements on competitive interviews since the population of competitors is much smaller than that of customer market. It is possible to interview 100 percent of the population of competitors except some unique markets with low entry barrier or very fragmented market such as Chinese coating market with over 8,000 players.

This measurement is suggested to be conducted by competitive interviews over the telephone interviews. Sometimes face-to-face interview is more adopted since it is a touching approach to sit the respondent to talk if the respondent overreacts to talk such sensitive issue. The interviewee is not willing to share the market intelligence to their best knowledge when he doesn't know the interviewer well or the questions are too sensitive. Some cardinal questions can be taken are:

- Company unit shipments in 200X?
- Sales in U.S. dollars?
- The estimated market share?
- The market share of key competitors?
- The estimated total market size?
- Market share winner and loser?
- Product price?

Obviously, many respondents will not answer all of these questions posed in this manner and this order. Appropriate asking order and response rate should be taken by blending them into a very free-form and smooth conversation and by style of sharing information with each other. For example, the interviewee might be told what one of the key competitors feels about the company or its sales; what an expert in professional association comment on the company revenue; what main stream media report the company market share; and what a marketing research company concludes about its competitor's situation etc. This usually gets them involved.

Alluring questions on market general and competitive landscape of total market can be forestalled to seize the attention of respondents and impress them that they are talking with a market researcher, not an economic spy employed by competitors and they will have much acquisition about market from talking.

It is also important to build a verification process into the interviewing strategy. Some of the respondents will be stumped. They don't know the correct answers, or may not tell the truth. A verification strategy will help eliminate such problems.

A verification strategy entails interviewing multiple people in the same organization to cross check sales figures, and by asking competitors their opinions about the accuracy of the responses received. The alternative is also attempted to multiply the average price of the unit by the unit sales to see if it matches the dollar sales given in the interview.

Once all interviews completed, a chart like that in Figure 3.12 can be concluded.

Figure 3.12 Market Share: Measurement Example (Competitors approach)

Company	Revenue (2004) ($ Million)	M/S by Value (%)	Volume (2004)	M/S by Volume (%)	$\Delta M/S_{(Value-Volume)}$
A	18	2.2	34,500	3.8	<0
B	50	6.0	91,000	9.9	<0
C	102	12.5	114,000	12.5	=0
Others	650	79.3	676,500	73.8	>0
Total	820	100.0	916,000	100.0	-

Note: All figures are rounded.

From the sales figures and the total market size, you can calculate market share.

End-users analysis

The other group you can interview or survey to make a market share calculation is the customer group. Various approaches such as telephone survey, mail survey, and trade show interviews can be adopted to mark market share calculation.

The disadvantage with customer interviews is the huge population. To get a fairly accurate estimate of market share, interviews as many as possible need to be performed on the best efforts. Also, the estimate of market share is usually based on installed units in use and not a specific year of sales, so it is difficult to measure the market share of new entries into the market. Their relative importance will be greatly diminished and receding.

To avoid this, a questionnaire with standardized questions must be designed and tested. The following are some key points should be touched:
- Purchased units of the specific product on year basis?
- Purchased brands or product types on year basis?
- Current using brands?

Figure 3.13 illustrates a sample of the consolidated responses from this survey and shows how to calculate the market share from the responses.

Figure 3.13 Market Share: Measurement Example (End-users Method)

Company	Product	Using Population	M/S Installed Base (%)	Purchasing Population (2004)	M/S (2004) (%)
A	x	1,025	35.4	82	23.1
B	y	821	28.3	68	19.2
C	z	553	19.1	124	35.1
Others	x+y+z	500	17.2	80	22.6
Total	x+y+z	2,899	100.0	354	100.0

Note: All figures are rounded.

You can also see that company C is probably a newcomer to the market because its share of the installed base is less than their market share based on new customer orders in 2004.

This is not the best method to calculate market share, but it does provide some valuable strategic information.

Case Study: Air-refresher Manufacturer Perception

A pioneer air-refresher manufacturer jump-started a in-depth research in the global air-refresher market. The research company was commissioned to provide a snap-shot of the total market general and insightful analysis on its major competitors.

The analysts of research company discovered that the firm was one of ten truly international companies selling air-refreshers and was clearly the market leader in sales volume and product technology.

A strategic research plan was tailored for making accurate measurement. The initial work was commenced internally within the company to learn everything that the company managers knew about the market for air-refreshers. By a simple technique, interview responses from the 30 managers were averaged. Two key findings were that the company market share was believed between 70 percent and 80 percent, that the world market was projected at just over $200 million, and that 10 manufacturers were identified by their awareness.

Cross-check was taken next to verify the data reliability. As often happens, the preliminary survey results showed that the managers had overestimated their share of the market and underestimated the size of the world market.

Also, several mistakes over the years that had cost them a tremendous amount of market share and sales were identified during survey:

Insufficient communication with people in the field. The firm's management would rarely spend time on international travel, in the field talking to employees, or communicating with customers and competitors.

- Lack of knowledge concerning principal competitors. At the study's completion, over 76 competitive manufacturers of air-refreshers that were selling into the same applications were identified. However, many of the competitors had less than $1 million in sales annually. But, despite their size or the quality of their products, they did contribute to the market.
- Lack of knowledge of customer preference. Local governments and universities were large customer group using many of local companies to supply homemade equipment to the local infrastructure, thus reducing imports of foreign-made equipment. Many governments were installing air-refreshers and preferred to have a local company supply it.
- Erroneous identification of market growth. The market was identified to be growing at approximately 5 percent per year (as were its sales), the company did not feel that a heavy investment in product R&D over the years to maintain market share was justified. Actually, it grows 15% annually. In the 1970s, when the firm pioneered the market, it dominated with a share of over 70 percent. However, by the time of research in 2004, the firm's market share had fallen to 20 percent of the world market and that share was continuing to fall because of the lack of R&D investment in the product development cycle, as shown in Figure 3.14

Figure 3.14 Market Share: Data Comparison

	Internal Survey	External Survey
M/S 2004 (%)	70-80	20
Competitor Population	10	76
Growth Rate (5-year average %)	5	15

Note: All figures are rounded.

Strategic recommendations:

- Shift from a confused global strategy to a segmented geographic strategy.
- Analyze each subsidiary in different region for competition and by customer base to determine what is needed to recapture market share.
- Make lobbying efforts on national governments to convince them that the cost of purchasing a more durable import product is less than using a poor quality local product.
- Increase R&D spending to develop a complete new manufacturing line with more options and excellent packaging.
- Fine-tune price to fit each country's market, and restaff sales forces to match actual market potential.

Market Potential

Definition

The market potential is defined as "the limit approached by market demand as industry marketing effort goes to infinity, for a given environment [1, p.230]." Included in this definition is the concept of market demand: "Market demand for a product is the total volume that would be bought by a defined customer group in a defined geographical area in a defined time period in a defined marketing environment under a defined marketing program," [1, p.228]. So the market potential can be epitomized into eight factors. Notably, each factor is also as concept with generally accepted definitions in the marketing literature.

- Product
- Total volume
- Be bought
- Customer group
- Geographical area
- Time period
- Marketing environment
- Marketing program

The network of eight related concepts gives meaning to the concept of market potential and provides a basis for measurement. By operationalizing each factor with specific measures, the value ultimately assigned to market potential can be qualified for analytical and strategic purposes.

In effect, the eight factors defining the concept of market potential provide the basis for a disciplined way to investigate and explain differences and similarities in forecasts. [2] Nevertheless, market potential is different from a market forecast in that a forecast is typically performed on a product or market segment that already exists. Market potential is typically the measurement of how much the market can absorb of a given product in the future.

Market engineering system can not be applied where no market exists. It is certainly correct to say that this type of market engineering is more difficult. The lack of a market for a new product often simple means that there is no competition yet. The diligent market engineer focuses on potential customers, which can be identified through advanced research techniques.

An accurate estimate of the market potential is very important because on this measurement a lot of investments in product development, production capacity, and marketing tools can be determined.

Because this measurement is typically used in markets that do not currently exist, it is important to use it as a gauge from which to determine the magnitude and speed of future investments.

The list below illustrates some applications of this measurement:

- Gauge size of R&D budget
- Gauge size of marketing environment
- Indicate degree to which competition will a attracted
- Help set sales forecasts
- Help attract outside investors
- Help with production planning

Methods of Measurement

Several methods for estimating sales potential are available. The primary methods are outline below.

- End-user surveys

  End-user surveys can be performed to measure market potential. These can be particularly useful when trying to measure the market potential for a product that does not currently exist. The key to these interviews is to explain adequately to the interviewee how the product will work, the benefits of the product or service, and what it will cost. If this is done properly, you can get a fairly good idea of what the market potential will be by asking respondents if they would buy and how many they would buy over time.

- Purchase proportion

  A purchase proportion-based measurement is one in which you compare the sales of the product under investigation to sales of a related market or product segment. This is useful with a new product serving as an add-on device to work with an existing product, or when the product can replace an existing product on the market. If there are 10,000 units installed of a given device that can easily be replaced by the new invention, one could argue that there will be a 1:1 replacement rate that therefore the market potential is 10,000 units.

■ Correlative indexes

Correlative indexes are used to determine the relative market potential of different market segments. The calculation is based on the premise that when one series of data demonstrates a significant degree of correlation to another, the first may be used to estimate the second. The second is the product or service on which you are taking the measurement.

Have-buy Model

Measuring market potential requires extensive marketing research effort and measurement methods differ widely. The customer group comprises a very large variety of firms of all sizes. Nevertheless, there exists a practical and effective approach to measure the market potential that is called "Have-buy Model" shown in Chart 3.12 It does not cover or apply to products that are radically new and have never been used by any of the participants in the marketplace. It is the most useful when applied to established products with potentially expanding markets at any given time However, they can equally be used, with only minor modifications, for mature products the demand for which has leveled off or is actually declining.

The current existing market can be identified to comprise "Customer"s on installed base with 3 customer categories: have product, have similar, and have dissimilar, which is reflected in the customer triangle. "Have Product" represents that the current customers use products supplied by suppliers; "Have similar" is defined that the customers currently use the products supplied by competitors; "Have dissimilar" represents that the customers use the products in different categories. For instance, one customer uses industrial reducers made by company A and its competitors. So this customer is identified as both "Have Product" and "Have similar". If it also uses hydraulic system as well but company A does not produce, it is regarded as "Have dissimilar". Obviously, the purchased volume of customer categories of both "Have Product" and "Have Similar" indicate the market size. [6,7]

Likewise, similar to the customer triangle, the "Noncutomer" is plotted in non-cutomer circle consisting of 4 categories of no intention to buy, buy product, buy similar and buy dissimilar. "Noncustomer" is defined as potential customers who have or do not have intention to buy any products in different product categories offered by either suppliers or competitors. It is easily to understand that the combination of "Buy Product" and "Buy Similar" is the indicator of market potential.

Chart 3.12 Market Potential: Have-buy Model

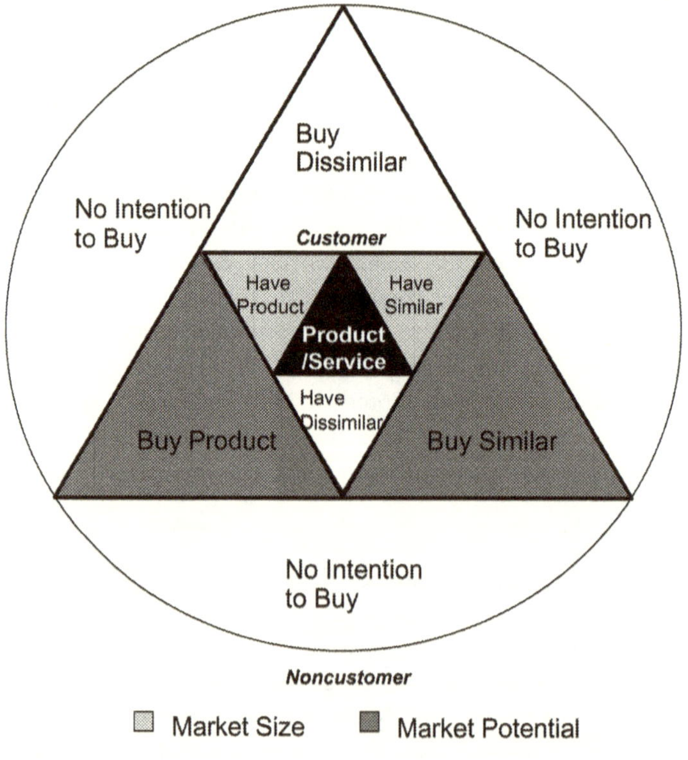

A six-step approach has been developed to provide a effective guide to determine market potential use "Have-buy Model" discussed shown in Chart 3.13. It is summarized, in a somewhat simplified and condensed form, as follows:

1. Identify the firm's present customer

   Establish a complete list of the customers in various market segments actively engaged in purchasing the product and to create the customer triangle.

2. Identify "Buy Product" category

   Use appropriate secondary data sources and approach to both existing customer and potential customer to ask if they have new purchasing plan and to identify one of the noncustomer categories "Buy Product" regardless of purchase proportion within the marketing territory. Most useful among published sources are directories of manufacturers published annually by many state governments or private organizations within states.

3. Identify "Buy Similar" category

   Extend the search to both existing customers and potential customers who tend to buy similar products but not identical in market segments to uncover noncustomer category of "Buy Similar" regardless of purchase proportion within market segments.

4. Identify "Buy Dissimilar" category

   Identify noncustomers within market segments dissimilar and unrelated to those presently supplied by your company. Rigorous interviews can be set up for a wide spectrum of knowledgeable individuals. In practice, little resistance is encountered in interview, and this approach has been proved successful and effective.

5. Separate "No Intention to Buy" from noncustomer categories.

   Use the same approach (the questioning of knowledgeable individuals as well as the use of secondary data sources) to identify noncustomers in three categories who, on account of the product they make or the service they perform, could not use the product/similar/dissimilar or have no purchasing plan. This approach has to be preceded by an investigation and analysis on both the potential user's product(s) and manufacturing process, and usually requires that interviews have certain amount of technical knowledge and competence.

6. Sum up "Buy Product" and "Buy Similar"

   The potential purchase volume of both "Buy Product" and "Buy Similar" is a good indicator of market potential. As to the "Buy Dissimilar", a potential marketing opportunity for suppliers is to seek for replacement. The "Buy

Dissimilar" could become customers after the product has been modified or buy existing product to replace the dissimilar. The "Buy Dissimilar" willing to take substitution shall be included.

Chart 3.13 Market Potential: A six-step approach to determine market potential

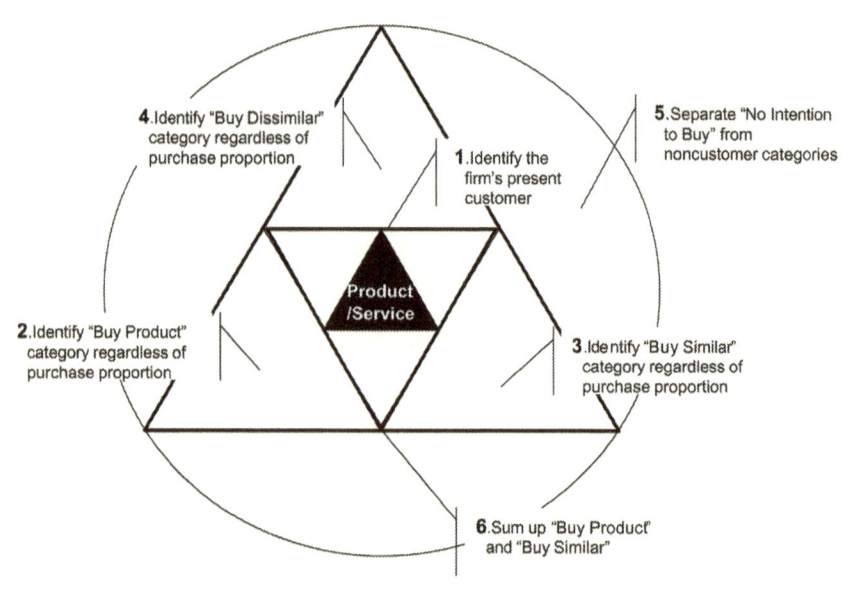

Besides the measuring market potential, it might be wise to calculate the market size from customer perspective. The total annual consumption by present customers includes the amount supplied by supplier as well as those supplied by competitors. To approach existing customers is probably the easiest way towards expanding the present sales volume. This may sound elementary or, perhaps, even superfluous to some industrial marketers. But is has been demonstrated, in practice, that this may well prove to be a highly rewarding approach. However, salesmen calling on such customers have often proved to be a rather unreliable source of information of customer product usage. Over the years, a great many formal approaches have been developed to improve such information gathering. They range all the way from formalized reporting systems (not mere call reports) involving salesmen with their information being cross-checked by line management as well as staff technical and marketing research specialists, to inspection visits to customer plants by specialists. The latter are frequently able to estimate a plant's annual consumption of a given product within fairly close limits.

Case Study: Anesthetic Gas Monitor

Several years ago, a medical electronics firm had developed an excellent device that accurately monitored the flow and absorption of anesthetic gases into the patient's blood during a surgical procedure.

The product represented a foray into a new market for the company, one about which it knew nothing. The firm requested a market study to assess that market-place for the product as a means of projecting sales.

The market potential was rosy and the company's reaction was predictably excited. It was experienced in dealing with instruments that sold in units of 100 to 200 per year. As a result, it lowered the sales estimate from 20,000 units per year to a more reasonable 200 units per year and went ahead with project development.

This was a crucial error in judgment. By reducing forecasted unit sales, the company was also effectively reducing the size of potential market, as illustrated in Figure 3.15.

By reducing the extent of the potential market for the new products, it also reduced its importance against other products it had in the R&D laboratory. Thus, with fewer resources allocated to this project, new product R&D duration was virtually doubled.

In hindsight, the company's actions were a grave mistake. The total market potential was so large that it was not missed by ten other manufacturers of medical equipment. All of them got products into the market before the medical firm. The net result was that the firm missed out on almost 4,000 potential unit sales of the instrument, constituting a loss in sales of $40,000,000 over a period of three years. It also relinquished the position of market leader owing to its comparatively late product introduction.

Figure 3.15 Market Potential: Original Calculation for Gas Monitoring Equipment

Measures	Formula	Calculation
Market Potential	= Number of operating rooms × 1 unit/operating room × unit price	= 80,000 (rooms) × 1 (unit) × $10,000 (price) = $800,000,000
Annual Market Potential	= Total Market Potential/ Number of years it will be sold before saturation	= $800,000,000/10 (years) = $80,000,000
Our Forecast for Client	= Estimated Market Share Obtainable × The annual market potential	= 25% x $80,000,000 = $20 Million/year = 2,000 units/year

Note: All figures are rounded.

Subsequent market engineering research revealed that competitors had stepped up their R&D efforts, bringing in almost three times the number of R&D engineers as the medical company had. It also reveals that the actual market size was not $80 million year per year but closer to $200 million per year.

The underlying point to this calculation is that market potential should be used as a barometer to gauge the R&D and marketing expenses. It would have been a tremendously profitable investment for the firm to double its R&D budget to bring its product to market more quickly.

Market Concentration

Definition

Market concentration refers to the number of firms that sell a particular product or collection of closely related products in a market and to the distribution of the firm's sizes in terms of sales. Concentration is considered to be an important dimension of market structure because it is thought to determine both the market power of competitors and opportunities for consumer choice.

The measurement of market concentration is not very exciting if only statistic measurement for one certain time such as one year is taken. Dynamic measurement needs to be employed to observe the market change over time. True strategic insight into the market comes when this measurement is taken over several years and a clear trend line can be concluded.

When concentration increases over time, then it poses a threat to smaller companies since the competitors are getting stronger, so it is very important for smaller companies to do competitive benchmarking against the leaders in the market. They must find out why those companies are winning market share. In cases like these, several strategies can be followed, such as guerrilla warfare, follow-the-leader, or leave-the market strategies.

On the contrary, when concentration declines over time, the market is growing increasingly competitive. Most likely, more than five companies are competing to be in the top-three positions. In this case, it is important to identify the small companies that are gaining market share and why.

Methods of Measurement

Unfortunately, there exists no universally accepted method for measuring market concentration. However, although no ideal concentration index can exist, it is possible to make some restrictions on concentration index by specifying an ad hoc collection of rational properties all indices must satisfy.

A comprehensive set of eleven axioms on market concentration is listed below based on the significant contributions by industrial economic practitioners [8,9]:

(i)   A concentration index should be a one-dimensional measure.

(ii)   An increase in the cumulative share of the ith firm, for all i, ranking firms 1,2,...i...N in descending order of size, implies an increase in concentration.

(iii) Concentration in an industry should be independent of the size of that industry.

(iv)   The principle of transfers should hold. Concentration should increase if the share of any firm is increased at the expense of a smaller firm.

(v)   If all firms are divided into K equal parts then the concentration index should be reduced by a proportion $1/K$

(vi)   If there are N firms of equal size, concentration should be a decreasing function of N.

(vii) The entry of new firms below some arbitrary significant size should reduce concentration.

(viii) Mergers should increase concentration.

(ix)   Random brand-switching by consumers should reduce concentration.

(x)   If s_j is the share of a new firm, then as s_j becomes progressively smaller so should its effect on a concentration index.

(xi)   Random factors in the growth of firms should increase concentration.

K-firm concentration ratio

The oldest and most commonly used of all indices is the K-firm concentration ratio, defined as the cumulative share of the Kth firm. More formally, using s_i to denote the share of the ith firm, we may define

$$CRK = \sum_{i=1}^{K} s_i$$

It is extremely simple to calculate, but the choice of K is somewhat arbitrary (for studies of aggregate concentration K is frequently taken to be 100; for market concentration values between 3 and 8 are usually employed). The index is simple one point on the cumulative concentration curve and so it may neglect important information. The major drawback of this index is that it does not reflect the size distribution of the K largest firms. Furthermore, it does not incorporate any information about the firms not included in this group of K largest firms.

The concept of the marginal concentration ratio was introduced to eke out the weakness of K-firm concentration ratio [10] which suggested to combine the market shares of the fifth to eighth largest firms including alongside CR4 as an important element of market structure. However, little is gained by doing this because the two concentration measures are closely related [11]. An inappropriate choice of K means that the above sets of axioms may not be satisfied. This is particularly true of the principle of transfers since the concentration ratio is not affected by changes outside the largest K firms if no firm disappears in the process. Such difficulties may be avoided by using a range of values for K, but interpretation of results becomes difficult if conflicting results emerge.

Hirschman-Herfindahl index

Hirschman-Herfindahl index is a frequently used index by researchers, defined as the sum of the squared market share values of all firms in a market. It is sometimes referred to as the Hirschman-Herfindahl index due to the disputation of the 'paternity' of the index. [12,13]

$$HHI = \sum_{i=1}^{f} S_i^2$$

It satisfies all of the summarized eleven axioms, and unlike the concentration ratio, depends on the share of each firm. The squaring of the market shares makes the contribution to the HHI of the bigger firms disproportionately large, reflecting the assumption that the largest firms in a market have disproportionate market power.

The calculated values of the HHI are not particularly intuitive, ranging between 0 and 10,000 by definition. A rule of thumb has been established for the HHI as follows:

- HHI < 1,000 Unconcentrated market
- 1,000 < HHI Moderately concentrated market
- 1,800 < HHI Highly concentrated market

This rule of thumb might not be appropriate, however, for industries in which there are a limited number of competitors to begin with [17].

Entropy

Entropy index has various scientific interpretations, but to a statistician it measures the information that is implied by the shape of a probability, or frequency, distribution. If, for example, the probabilities for the whole range of possible values of a variable are all equal, the implication is that little or no specific information is available. Entropy can also be regarded as a measure of the uncertainty of firms about their market shares. In its simplest, first order form, it is measured by

$$E = -\sum_{i}^{N} s_i \log s_i$$

Which for a given number of firms, N, takes its maximum value of log N where firms' shares are equal. At the other extreme E is zero if there is only one firm. The higher the value of E, therefore, the lower the level of concentration, and vice versa. An advantage of the entropy measure is that if there are distinct sub-groups of firms, it can be decomposed into within-group and between-group entropies.

If E is divided by its maximum value an index of relative entropy is produced which is constrained to lie between zero and 1 [14]. A weakness of this index is that it might not register an increase in concentration when mergers take place, because although mergers reduce the value of E, implying that concentration has increased, there may be a proportionately greater fall in $logN$, so that relative entropy increases, thus implying a fall in concentration.

Absolute concentration

The mean of the so-called 'first moment distribution' of firms's sizes [15]. This is given by

$$\overline{X}_I = \sum x_i H$$

Where x_i are firms' sizes and H denotes the Herfindahl index.

This amounts to applying the Herfindahl index to absolute sizes as opposed to firms' shares, giving what they call an 'absolute concentration' index [16].

Rosenbluth index

The Rosenbluth index [17] is defined as

$$R = \frac{1}{2\sum is_i - 1}$$

i.e. firms' shares are weighted by their rank positions. The index measures the area above the concentration curve the satisfies all of the Hall-Tideman axioms [8], but not Hannah and Kay s fourth axiom [9] concerning the effects of mergers.

Comprehensive concentration index

The 'comprehensive concentration index' [18] is defined as

$$CCI = s_1 + \sum_{i=2}^{N} s_i^2 (2 - s_i)$$

Where s_1 is the share of the largest firm.

The index is similar to twice the Herfindahl index minus the sum of the cubes of firms' shares, except that greater weight is assigned to the share of the largest firm. It is intended to reflect both the relative size of the largest firm and the dispersion by size of all firms in the distribution, but it may not satisfy the principle of transfers.

Market concentration is important in so far as it influences business behaviour, so that the most appropriate measure of concentration is the one that is most closely related to behaviour. However, the complexity of business life is such that in practice it is unlikely that there is one concentration measure which will clearly be superior in all circumstances. For instance, if industry behavior is dominated by the five leading firms who have regard for each other's competitive responses but ignores smaller insignificant competitors, then the five firm concentration ratio will be closer approximation to the reality of business behaviour than say the Herfindahl index which gives some weight to all the firms in an industry. On the other hand, if small firms have an important influence on general industry behaviour this influence will not be captured by the concentration ratio.

Case Study: Information Industry Concentration

Aimed to an opening of market to competitors and a reduction of market power, the government telecommunication department has issued liberalization policies to deregulate the telecommunications and electronic mass media market to encourage competition.

Several decades later, the authority wants to know the impact of these liberalization policies on competitive market structure. Bearing this mind that industry concentration is the response to competition; a in-depth research on the concentration in telecommunications and related industries needs to be taken. Obviously, all parts of the information sector are subject to structural change due to technology, convergence, and other factors. Hence the problem can be refined as follows:

■ How has liberalization policy affected market structure?

■ What has been the trend of concentration in the regulated segments of the telecom industry (and of other regulated media industries), in comparison to unregulated parts of the information sector?

To provide an empirical answer, the market concentration trends of differentiated segments are investigated, such as long distance telecommunications, cellular mobile, broadcast TV, cable TV, film distribution, daily newspaper, Internet service providers, etc. For each segment, individual firms' market shares and revenues are tracked and calculated based on a variety of sources. These market shares were then used to calculate concentration indices and to track them over time. The major concentration index used was the Herfindahl-Hirschman Index (HHI). The concentration indices starting from the year 1996 were tracked which experienced a significant deregulatory law. Then the indices of different segments were aggregated along the dimensions of broader sectors such as telecom, mass media and internet and along the dimension of regulated/unregulated industries. The weighted aggregate HHI is defined as

$$WAHHI = \sum_{j=1}^{n} \frac{m_j}{\sum m_j} \sum_{i=1}^{f} S_{ij}^2$$

Where j = a segmented industry
  m_j = toal revenue of a segmented industry
  S_i = each firm's market share of a segmented industry
  n = number of segments in a specific sector
  f = number of firms in a segmented industry.

The research framework of this project is presented in Chart 3.14 with horizontal and vertical comparison. Three major sectors are segmented for total information industry:

■ Telecom
■ Mass Media
■ Internet

For each of those sectors, three categories of industries were defined:

■ Regulated
   Ex: local telecommunications, TV stations
■ Unregulated but closely affected by regulation
   Ex: fiber optic cables, cable TV channels
■ Unregulated
   Ex: film distribution, fax machines

Chart 3.14 Market Concentration: Research Framework

Vertical Comparison

Chart 3.15 Market Concentration: HHI Concentration in Telecom Sectort

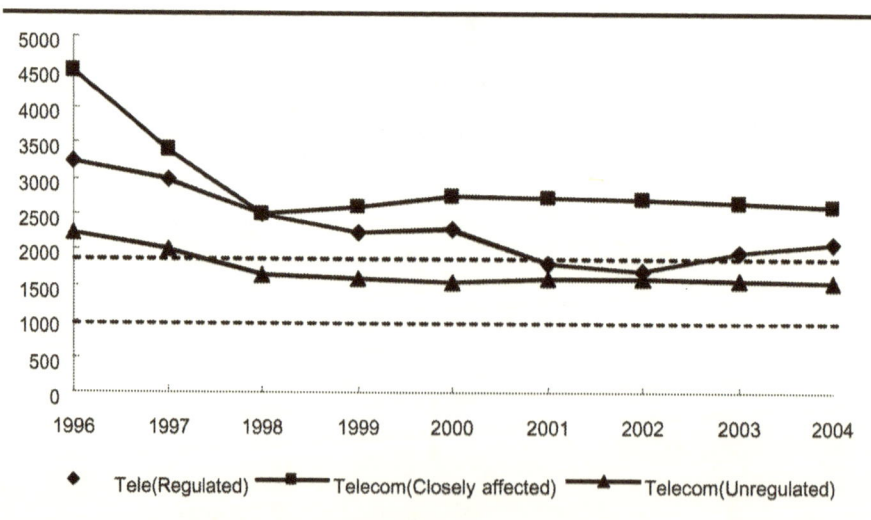

Note: All figures are rounded.

A competitive landscape of information industry was generated for government. For instance, the concentration of telecom sector is featured in Chart 3.15

Unregulated telecom industries decline in concentration in the 2nd half 1990s, and are flat when stepping into 2000s. Their concentration is intermediate in size. Unregulated industries that are materially affected, mostly in equipment markets like fiber optics and wireless infrastructure, show roughly the same trends, except that their concentration level is much higher, they drop rapidly after 1996. Most of these industries are providing telecom equipment, and they are dominated by a handful of vendors.

But most interesting is the concentration trend of early regulated telecom industries: from highly concentrated in the early 1996, concentration levels decline especially with the liberalization policies issued, until 2002. In that year, the concentration level is at its lowest, though barely touching the bottom range of high concentration, and it thereafter abruptly turns back to higher concentration levels.

Conclusively, the government policies do have poignant negative effect on market power and has stimulated the market competition at the early stage. Whereas, at the end of one business cycle like observed after 2002, competition is giving way to consolidation. The traditional system of regulated market power and concentration has returned to some new equilibrium level which is not the hoped-for competition but some market power. Thus it is the right time for government to rethink about the marketing strategies upon current scenario and reality.

Market Saturation

Definition

A frequent theme in discussions of market saturation is an implicit comparison of the current level of market output for a particular good with the potential level of market output [19]. The potential (maximum) output is commonly considered to be the cumulative result of a general pattern of growth and decay which affects every good so that a period of expanding output (and purchase) is inevitably followed by contraction. Any explicit comparison of potential with current output requires an operational definition of the potential output level. One well-known approach which makes an implicit comparison of actual and potential outputs is the fitting of secular growth curves to historical time series shown in Chart 3.16

Chart 3.16 Market saturation: Comparison of actual and potential outputs

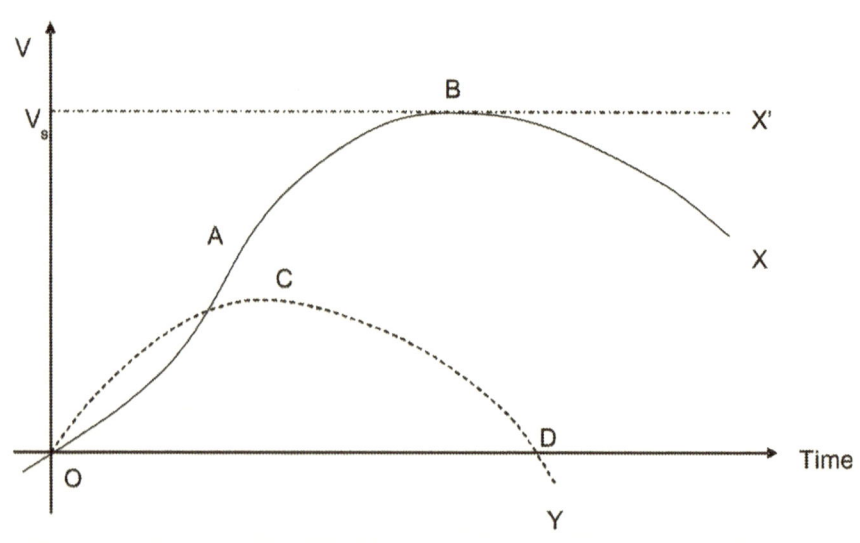

Where OX = potential growth curve
V_sX' = saturation level
OY = actual growth curve
A = inflection point
B = saturation point

The typical expected growth pattern is one of increasing then decreasing rates of growth finally terminating in zero or negative rates. The point at which peak output is reached is often called the saturation point [20]. For a good whose output follows such a time path, the level or state of market saturation occurs at the point(s) in time defined by inequality (1):

$$NP_t \le NP_{t-1} \qquad (1)$$

where NP_t is the level of new purchases in period t.

According to (1) a market is saturated (reaches a state of saturation) when current new purchases are less than or equal to those of the preceding period. The time period represented by t can be weighted averages of current and past values to avoid short run exogenous disturbances. Rather than this static definition, it may be more useful to specify (1) in terms of rates of change rather than absolutes or levels. The percentage change or growth counterpart of (1) can be written as:

$$gNP_t \le gNP_{t-1}$$

where g signifies that the variable is measured as a proportional rate of change. If the percentage change of new purchases in the current period is less than that of the previous period, the market is said to be saturated. This dynamic definition of saturation can be interpreted as the movement of a particular market toward or away from the state of saturation defined.

Market saturation rate

In market research, market saturation is when the quantity of products in use in the market place is close to or at its maximum. The market saturation rate is defined as the degree to which the end-user base is currently using the given product or service. It is calculated by dividing the current number of users by the total potential number of users.

$$R_s = \frac{N_c}{N_p}$$

Where R_s = market saturation rate
   N_c = number of current users
   N_p = number of potential users

The saturation rate represents the approximate age of the market or product segment. A fully saturated market is most likely in the mature stage of the product life cycle, and an appropriate marketing strategy should be chosen. If the saturation rate is low, the product is usually assumed in the infant or introduction phase of the life cycle. However, that some products can reach the maturity stage and never achieve a saturation rate above 10 percent. As in any diagnostic procedure, several measurements must be made for a proper diagnosis of the market.

The saturation rate of the market should have a profound impact on the product development and marketing strategy. Figure 3.16 serve as an example.

Figure 3.16 Market saturation: Market/Product Strategy vs. Saturation Rate

Saturation Rate	Market Strategy	Product Strategy
Low (0%~25%)	Large investments into the 8 marketing tools. Customer education might be important. Focusing on developing a customer base is key to success.	Development of product upgrades. Investment is low.
Medium (25%~75%)	Investment in marketing is stable. Competitive-based strategy is now more important.	Development of product upgrades and new version. Investment in R&D is more important.
High (75%~100%)	Marketing investment is reduced. Competition is high. Price could be important.	R&D lab now needs to have a product replacement or a new technology in progress or soon to be released.

When a market is saturated, it will be growing primarily on product replacement. Most likely, the marketing strategy will need to be very competitively oriented, with a focus on new benefits and features.

The market saturation rate also will give some insight on how to forecast the market's future growth. Obviously, highly saturated markets will be growing on average more slowly than markets with low saturation rates. And, as stated earlier, one should realize that not all markets will reach 100 percent saturation. For example, cellular car telephones are very popular, and the market is growing very quickly. However, it is not expected ever to reach even 75 percent saturation of the potential customer base.

Replacement & upgrading

In most markets there is a limit to the number of items which the market is likely or able to buy. When the saturation point is reached supplying organizations must rely on replacement business where items in use in the market have to be replaced as they get old, perhaps malfunction or when users want to upgrade to a later version of the item. Further producers have to compete more aggressively with alternate companies because there are no new users left to the market and everyone will have become someone's customer. This inevitably means that sales volumes can be reduced from their level as the market was being penetrated with people buying their first example of that item.

Clever marketers will always try to ensure that there are significant upgrade benefits to try to persuade the population of owners of a product that they should buy a later version rather than keep their original item. There are many examples in the markets for mobile phones, for personal computers and their software and for cars, a continual struggle to maintain persuasive reasons for past customers to buy a newer version.

Tied to this concept of market saturation and drivers for upgrading is the idea of planned or built in obsolescence where the maker of an item plans that at some point in the future it will loose its value, become faulty or its life will come to an end. Light bulbs are a good example here, for not much more money you could buy a light bulb which would last pretty much indefinitely but this would reduce the value of the repurchase market to the manufacturers. To be fair to light bulb manufacturers the expected lifetime of their products is getting longer so the effect in this market is not so noticeable. [21]

Methods of Measurement

The two methodologies from which can be chosen to make this measurement are:

■ Competitive interviews combined with secondary research

To measure the saturation rate based on the competitor methodology contains two steps:

1) Calculate the total number of potential customers in the market.

   For certain products, it is helpful to calculate these figures by country or some other segmentation scheme to see differences in saturation rates among segments. Typically, the most efficient way to obtain these figures is by using secondary research techniques. It is relatively easy to find statistics in published sources on the number of end-users for virtually any of the products we research.

2) Interview competitors to calculate the total installed base of products in the market.

   This can be done by asking each competitor for its total scales of the product over time.

To verify your statistics, following questions might be asked for each of the competitor:

- How many units of product have been sold since its introduction?
- What is the estimated total installed base of this product?
- How large is the estimated total end-user base?
- What is the approximate market saturation?

By discussing the market saturation rate with each of the competitors, market researchers can get a better feeling for the accuracy of the measurement. This verification technique should be used on all measurements when possible.

- End-user interviews

The other methodology used to measure market saturation is surveying the potential customer population. This can be done over the telephone or with a mail survey.

The key factor with this methodology is to perform surveys on sample sizes that are large enough to provide accurate measurements of market saturation. It is also important to ensure that the surveys or interviews are done on the potential customer base and not just on current end-users. Failing to do this can lead to significant error.

To calculate market saturation, market researchers will need to ask potential end-users if they are currently using the product or services in question. Once the responses are received for an appropriate sample size, the market saturation rate can be calculated as follows:

$$S_M = \frac{N_{rc}}{N_r}$$

Where S_M = market saturation

N_{rc} = total number of respondents that use product

N_r = total number of respondents

Case Study: Kidney Stone Lithotriptor

One of the most exciting and revolutionary developments in medical technology in recent years was the kidney-stone lithotriptor, developed by the European firm Dornier.

The "kidney-stone crusher" was used to remove kidney stones from patients non-invasive using an electroshock focused on the region of the stone. The stone would be shattered by the shock and would pass naturally through the patient. This was a major breakthrough because up to that time a kidney-stone operation meant major surgery and weeks in the hospital. Today, owing to this machine, it has become an outpatient procedure.

One competitor was right behind Dornier in developing a similar device. The firm wanted to know if it had a chance of capturing any share of the market from Dornier. The market for these devices is ultimately limited by the number of patients requiring the procedure.

The critical measurement to take in this market would be the market saturation point for this product. The dynamic variables needed to be observed carefully were:

- Number of kidney-stone patients per year
- Number of larger hospital capable of purchasing the machine
- Geographic distribution of patients and hospitals
- Installed base of kidney-stone lithotriptors and booked-order backlog

Some required data was easily found on the medical reports from hospitals and statistics bureau shown in Figure 3.17. The next step is to calculate the market saturation rate. To make saturation rate, two variables need to be identified. One is current customer population; the other is potential customer population. The current customer can be determined as the hospital currently using kidney-stone lithotriptor, in other words, the hospitals on installed base. The potential customers can be identified as larger hospital has purchase power. There exist some other factors to be considered such as whether these hospitals have purchase demand of kidney-stone lithotriptor which largely depends on the patient population in geographic region; how patients and hospitals were distributed nationally because the machines need to be within 200 miles of the patient which could determine if there were any national regions that showed considerable potential, etc.

Then further interviews were conducted with hospitals with relatively large sample size to identify the purchasing potential. The market saturation rate calculations were shown in Figure 3.18

Figure 3.17 Market Saturation: Collected raw data

	Kidney-stone Patients Population 2004	Kidney-stone Lithotriptor Population 2004	Hospital Population 2004
State A	9,830	222	2,050
State B	5,649	145	2,152
State C	27,335	505	2,559
State D	27,924	370	2,545
State E	16,251	56	2,085
State F	6,514	129	1,610
...	...	...	...

Note: All figures are rounded.

Figure 3.18 Market Saturation: Transferred market data

	Hospital Population 2004	Hospital percent (purchase power) 2004	Hospital Percent (purchase demand) 2004	Potential Customer	Current Customer	Saturation Rate
State A	2,050	30%	50%	308	222	72.2%
State B	2,152	50%	15%	161	145	89.8%
State C	2,559	60%	45%	691	505	73.1%
State D	2,545	25%	80%	509	370	72.7%
State E	2,085	7%	60%	88	56	63.9%
State F	1,610	30%	30%	145	129	89.0%
...	...	...	...	...	...	...

Note: All figures are rounded.

It is profusely important phased work is to conduct an in-depth competitive analysis for Dornier. Since Dornier is the market practitioner and dominator, benchmarking Dornier can provide substantial market insights.

Dornier did something very clear in the early stages of market development As the first competitor in the market, the company had to penetrate the market as quickly as possible because it knew other manufacturers would see the market potential and rush into the market. Dornier maintained very high profit margin on the product and was aware of nine other manufacturers that were engaging in R&D.

To penetrate the market as rapidly as possible, Dornier developed a tremendous amount of excitement around its product, creating such fervor that hospitals were actually competing for the next delivery. Dornier's marketing strategy was brilliant. The firm created a massive demand and then made clients wait for a position on its installation timetable.

At the high point of sales, Dornier had a two-year delivery backlog. To get on the delivery schedule, customers had to make a noncancelable order with a 50 percent down payment. This locked potential competitors out of the market.

An interview with Dornier revealed that the market potential for its current instrument was about 500 units based on the total number of kidney procedures. A hospital has to make money on its $1 million investment, particularly with the diagnostic related group (DRG) system of reimbursement. DRGs limit what hospitals can charge for certain operations. Hospitals had to be sure that there was an adequate supply of patients within the geographic region to justify the expense.

The market saturation rate calculation showed that the market is averagely 76.8 percent saturated in 2004. Dornier had already closed future orders in virtually bigger cities. It becomes very clear that the kidney-stone lithotriptor market has stepped into high saturation stage and the wise competitors will think about withdrawing from current market or upgrading products.

Strategic recommendations

- Stop development of the kidney-stone lithotriptor since the market is saturated and it would be extremely difficult to break into such an established and saturated market.
- Examine innovations and new applications for the technology.
- Try to tap on the small cities since that is possibly the only opportunity left by Dornier at the time.

Market Attractiveness

Definition

Market attractiveness is a measure of the potential of the marketplace to yield growth in sales and profits. It is important to stress that this should be an objective assessment of market attractiveness using data external to the organization. The criteria themselves will, of course, be determined by the organization carrying out the exercise and will be relevant to the objectives that organization is trying to achieve, but it should be independent of the organization's position in its markets [22].

An important factor in determining success or failure of business firms is the selection of the right markets or market niches to be targeted. It is crucial to be able to generate the product mix optimally adapted to both the structure of the producers and the properties of the industry environment and demand schedule. Basically, the firm generates this mix either by imitative product diversification steps—entering existing markets—or by introducing product innovations into the market. In both cases the firm has to evaluate carefully the merits and risks of the new product it plans to add to its range.

The management literature has developed several standard approaches how to develop a useful evaluation of markets not covered by the current product range. The quintessence of these approaches is to identify some key factors that are important to estimate future profit possibilities on a market and to assign certain weights to these factors. A well known example is the GE approach (see e.g. Kottler (1997)) where market attractiveness is determined as the weighted sum of several factors. Among others, overall market size, market growth rate, historical profit margin and competitive intensity are the most important in the list. Clearly, the actual choice of the list of factors considered and in particular the weights assigned to the different factors is a strategic decision to be taken by the company. It will determine the firm's diversification strategy in general but also the approach towards product innovations in particular. A strong weight on market growth rates will lead companies to focus on young innovative markets. This comes with the risk of investing in markets which never take off or of neglecting established products with large current profitability. On the other hand, a strong focus on (historical) profits makes a firm vulnerable to missing new developments with respect to products or technology which might turn out to be essential for future success. This effect has been highlighted under the name 'Innovator's Dilemma' in Christensen (1997). Using several case studies he points out that leading companies in different markets have lost their industry leadership because they reacted too late to the existence of initially small and unprofitable but growing markets which eventually replaced their core business. One of the main reasons for their failure was that firms were focused on profit and revenues and existing business plans for these small but growing markets did not succeed internally to be implemented [23].

Methods of Measurement

An evaluation of the attractiveness of a particular market or market segment builds naturally on the kind of opportunity analysis. Market researchers can assess on the basis of information obtained from analyses of the environment and industry. To make this assessment, criteria need to be established against which prospective markets or market segments can be evaluated. Following are summarized key steps to conduct an assessment of market attractiveness:

Step 1: Define market attractiveness factors
Many of the factors that influence the organization's competitive position and the attractiveness of markets include the market's size and growth rate, various marketing environment factors—demographic, sociocultural, economic, political/legal, technological, and physical—that influence the demand in that market. An even more critical factor in determining whether to enter a new market or market segment, however, is the degree to which unmet customer needs, or needs that are currently not being well served, can be identified. In the absence of unmet or underserved needs, it is likely to be difficult to win customer loyalty, regardless of how large the market or how fast it is growing. "Me—too" products often face difficult going in today's highly competitive market [24]. Generally, market attractiveness stems from market forces, competition rivalry, customer power, and macro-environment factors. Diverse marketing environments of myriads of industry generate different factor system. Here are suggested factors contributing to market attractiveness:

1. Market forces
   - Size (value, volume, or both)
   - Key segment size
   - Total/segment growth rate
   - Market Diversity
   - Sensitivity of price, service etc.

- Technology substitution
- Cyclicity
- Seasonality
- Bargaining power of upstream suppliers
- Bargaining power of downstream suppliers

2. Competition rivalry
   - Competition structure
   - Degree of concentration
   - Degree of change
   - Entry and exist
   - Market share
   - Degree and type of integration

3. Customer power
   - Unmet needs
   - Undeserved needs
   - Customer loyalty
   - Price elasticity
   - Buyer concentration
   - Suppliers differentiation
   - Buyers backward integration

4. Macro-environment
   - Financial and economic (contribution margins, economies of scale, entry/exist barriers, capacity utilization etc)
   - Technological (maturity, volatility, complexity, differentiation, intellectual property, manufacturing etc)
   - Socio-political (attitudes and trends, regulations, restriction, culture etc.)
   - Demographic (personal preference, unionization, community acceptance etc.)
   - Environmental (environmental protection regulations etc.)

Step 2: Weight factors
A numerical weight is assigned to each factor to indicate its relative importance in the overall assessment. The factors can be classified into hierarchical system

shown in Figure 3.19. The sum of the weights assigned to the factors in the same level must be valued at 100%.

Figure 3.19 Market attractiveness: Calculation of market attractiveness index

Factor	Weight	Sub-factor	Weight	Rate (Not~Very =0~5)	Score	Overall Score
Market Forces	40%	Market size	60%	5	3.0	
		Growth rate	40%	2	0.8	
			100%		3.8	1.52
Competitive rivalry	30%	No. of competitor	30%	5	1.5	
		Entry and exist	20%	3	0.6	
		Degree of concentration	20%	1	0.2	
			100%		2.3	0.69
Customer power	20%	Customer loyalty	60%	2	1.2	
		Unmet needs	40%	5	2	
			100%		3.2	0.64
Macro-environment	10%	Technology complexity	20%	4	0.8	
		Environmental protection regulations	30%	5	1.5	
		Human factors	50%	3	1.5	
			100%		3.8	0.38
	100%					3.23

(Market attractiveness index)

Note: All figures are rounded.

Step 3: Rate factors

This step requires that evidence—typically both qualitative and quantitative data—be collected to objectively assess each of the criteria identified in Step 1.

Step 4: Calculate market attractiveness index

The market attractiveness index can be easily derived from calculating the total factor-weighted score as follows:

$$MA = \sum [W \times \sum (W_s \times R)]$$

Where **MA** = market attractiveness index
  W = weight of each factor
  W_s = weight of each sub-factor
  R = rate of each sub-factor

Chart 3.17 Market attractiveness: Four-step approach of market attractiveness evaluation

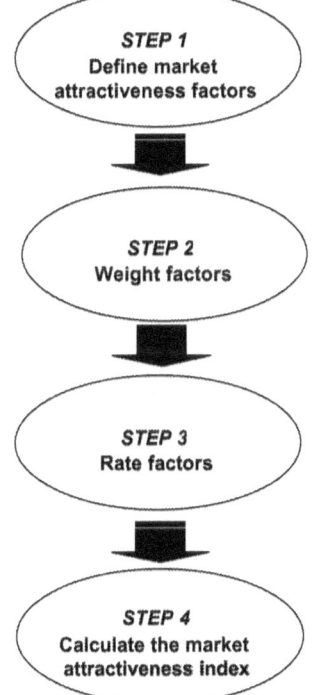

Case Study: Agriculture Machinery Products

One Japanese leading agriculture machinery manufacturer with 80 years history tends to expand its business into China which is one of the largest agriculture countries in the world. It believes the booming economy in China will stimulate the agriculture development with government support which brims over with potential opportunities for agriculture machinery manufacturers.

The company decided to take a insightful market research to help company better understand the agriculture machinery market in China to further build actionable market entry strategies. The market intelligence department has developed a comprehensive research process including detailed phased work with professional and conceptual market measurement. The market attractiveness is an essential measure employed to identify this market.

The market researchers provided a snapshot of China market with comparison with other regions across the world. The decision markers feel it is necessary to take a further step to dig into the detailed segments. China is a country with diversity and vitality because of numbers of ethical and culture difference by province. For in-depth perception of Chinese market, market analysts segmented China by geographic region to take longitudinal comparison of each province by attractiveness measuring factors.

First of all, the measuring factors were identified and then weights were assigned to each factor shown in Figure 3.20

Figure 3.20 Market Attractiveness: Factors to evaluate the agriculture machinery market

Attractiveness factor	Weight
Rural population (K persons)	10%
Cultivated lands (km²)	15%
Sales volume 2004 (units)	20%
Growth rate 2003-04	25%
Penetration rate (sales volume/rural population)	30%
	100%

Note: All figures are rounded.

The actual data for each region was obtained from association publications listed in Figure 3.21. Each region was rated according to the statistics. The overall rank was calculated by market attractiveness index formula. Here the rank was used to for calculation instead of the rate. The decision makers can judge the most attractive business region from this evaluation.

Figure 3.21 Market Attractiveness: Overall rank calculation

Region	Overall Rank	Rural population (K persons)	Cultivated Land (km²)	Sales Volume 2004	Growth Rate 2003~04	Penetration Rate
A	29	357.6	3,439	153	-31.4%	0.4
B	27	386.6	4,856	73	-60.8%	0.2
C	6	5,388.8	68,833	17,259	-11.8%	3.2
D	18	2,327.4	45,886	5,877	7.9%	2.5
E	23	1,370.0	82,010	12,067	11.8%	8.8
F	19	2,314.5	41,748	8,938	-1.9%	3.9
G	22	1,443.5	55,784	3,182	7.9%	2.2
H	21	1,890.5	117,730	17,454	10.8%	9.2
...	...	...	...	...	...	...

Note: All figures are rounded.

Replacement Rate

Definition

The replacement rate of a market is the rate at which customers replace either worn-out or outdated products with a new or improved product.

Rates of product replacement can tell the researchers a great deal about a market, particularly saturated markets that are highly contested. In a saturated market, new product sales are usually determined by the rate of replacement. As the installed base of the product becomes obsolete and users begin to upgrade, manufacturer's sales begin to increase. Thus, it behooves the astute market engineer to be well versed in the product replacement cycle for a particular market.

Methods of Measurement

Only one way to measure the replacement rate in a market is reliable, and that is by asking customers how often they replace the product, when they bought it, and when they next plan to replace it.

The equation below illustrates the equation to calculate the replacement rate of a market:

$$R_r = \frac{U_s - U_n}{B_c}$$

Where R_r is the replacement rate, U_s is the units sold in certain year, U_n is the units sold to new customers, B_c is the old customer base. The high replacement rate means the technology or product need to be considered to be substituted; the low replacement rate means the technology or product can be retained for existing customers.

To get an accurate calculation of the replacement rate, the researchers will need to survey a fairly large sample of end-users. Typically 100 to 1,000 will do for most high-technology markets. In surveying the end-user, you can use telephone interviews, personal interviews at trade shows, or mail surveys, Do not ask the sales force to find out since the salesperson will exaggerate it.

The key point in making this measurement is asking the right questions in the right way. Too often, an interviewer can bias the results or the questions can be misunderstood. Some sample questions might be:

- When did you purchase this type of product for the first time?
  - Month?
  - Year?
- When did you replace the product?
- If you still have the product, when do you expect to replace the product?
  - Month?
  - Year?
  - Never?
  - Don't know
- What will you need to see before you decide to replace the product?

The replacement rate is a very important measurement in mature markets because it tells the marketing people if most of the sales volume is coming from customers who are already using this technology. Knowing the most of the sales volume will be coming from replacement sales, the decision makers will want to set a different marketing strategy than if most of the sales were going to new customers.

New customers will typically need more education, support, and literature, while replacement customers are looking more for cost benefits, upgrade potential, customer support, and service.

If a market has a high replacement rate, that is 20 percent or more each year, the market researchers can typically conclude the either the products are not very reliable, are disposable, or that the technology is change very quickly, as in personal computers (PCs). The investor will need to keep the company very dynamic if the investor plan to be successful in these markets. There will be great pressure for continued product improvements.

If the replacement rate is very low, 5 percent or less per year, then the key strategy will most likely be looking for new customers because the customers who bought from the company last years will not need to be seen for another 20 years.

Notes and References

[1] R.G.Hamermesh, M. J. Anderson, Jr and J.E.Harris, Strategies for low market share business, Harvard Business Review, 56 (3), 95-105 (1978)

[2] Robert D. Buzzell, Bradley, T. and Ralf G.M.Sultan, Market share—a key to profitability, Hardvard Business Review, 53 (1), 97-106 (1975)

[3] B.K.Dutta and W.R.King, A competitive scenario modeling system, Management Science, 26 (3), 261-273 (1980)

[4] R.D.Buzzell and F.D.Wiersema, Successful share-building strategies, Harvard Business Review, pp. 135-144, January-February (1981)

[5] J.D.C.Little, Brandaid: a marketing-mix model, Operations Research, 23 (4), 628-672 (1975)

[6] Kotler, P. Marketing Management, 5th ed. Englewood Cliffs, NJ: Prentic-Hall, 1984.

[7] Robert J. Thomas, Forecasting New Product Market Potential: Combining Multiple Methods, Journal of Production Innovation Management, 4, pp.109-119 (1987)

[8] Hall, M. and Tideman, N., Measures of Concentration, Journal of the American Statistical Association, 62 (March 1967), pp. 162-68.

[9] Hannah, L. and Kav, J. A., Concentration in Modern Industry: Theory, Measurement and the U.K.Experience, (Macmillan, London, 1977)

[10] Miller, R.A. Marginal Concentration Ratios and Industrial Profit Rates: Some Empirical Results, Southern Economic Journal, XXXIV (October 1967), pp. 259-67

[11] Collins, N.R.and Preston, L.E., Price-Cost Margins and Industry Structure, Review of Economics and Statistics, 51 (August 1969), pp. 271-86

[12] Herfindahl, O. C., Concentration in the U.S. Steel Industry, (Unpublished thesis, Columbia University, New York, 1950)

[13] Hirschman, A.O., National Power and the Structure of Foreign Trade, (University of California Bureau of Business & Economic Research, Berkeley, 1945)

[14] Horowitz, A. R. and Horowitz, I., Entropy, Markov Processes and Competition in the Brewing Industry, Ijiri, Journal of Industrial Economics, 16 (July 1968), pp. 196-211

[15] Niethans, J., An index of the size of Industrial Establishments, International Economic Papers, 8 (1958), pp. 122-32

[16] Hannah, L. and Kav, J.A., Concentration in Modern Industry: Theory, Measurement and the U.K.Experience, (Macmillan, London, 1977).

[17] Utton, M.A. (1970) Industrial Concentration, Harmondsworth, Penguin Books.

[18] Horvath, J., A Suggestion for a Comprehensive Measure of Concentration, Southern Economic Journal, XXXVI, 4 (April 1970), pp. 446-52.

[19] Simon S. Kuznets, Secular Movements in Production and Prices (Boston: Houghton Mifflin Company, 1930), esp. Chapter II, and Harold T. Davis, The Analysis of Economic Time Series (Bloomington, Ind.: The Principia Press, Inc., 1941), Chapter 6, esp.pp.240-271.

[20] Lloyd J. Mercer and W. Douglas Morgan, Alternative interpretations of market saturation: Evaluation for the automobile market in the late twenties, Explorations in Economic History, Vol. 9, 1971-1972, pp. 269-290

[21] Market Saturation: defined by the Sticky-marketing.com monthly magazine (http://www.sticky-marketing.net) 17/08/2001

[22] Harper W. Boyd, Marketing management: A strategic Decision-making approach (4th Ed.), p. 207, Mcgraw Hill (2002)

[23] Herbert Dawid and Marc Reimann, Evaluating Market Attractiveness: Individual Incentives vs. Industrial Profitablity, Working paper No.62, Center for Empirical Macroeconomics

[24] Roger J. Best, Market-based Management: Strategies for growing customer value and profitability, p. 196, Prentice Hall (2004)

Chapter 4

Competitor Analysis

In formulating business strategy, managers must consider the strategies of the firm's competitors. While in highly fragmented commodity industries the moves of any single competitor may be less important, in concentrated industries competitor analysis becomes a vital part of strategic planning.

Competitor analysis has several important roles in strategic planning:

- To help management understand their competitive advantages/disadvantages relative to competitors
- To generate understanding of competitors' past, present (and most importantly) future strategies
- To provide an informed basis to develop strategies to achieve competitive advantage in the future
- To help forecast the returns that may be made from future investments (e.g. how will competitors respond to a new product or pricing strategy?

After giving some background about the type of competitors the firm's business will identify and analyze the major competitors—those most likely to impact on the success of firm business. The analysis uses a variation of SWOT, a popular strategic planning tool, to help identify strengths and weaknesses of competitors, and then opportunities and threats for own business.

Benefits of Competitor Analysis

- The company's competitive advantage can be discovered including the reasons customers do business with the company instead of the competitors.

It is suggested for the company to communicate the competitive advantage effectively to win potential customers.

- The ideas for innovative improvements to the product offerings can be generated from analyzing current issues and the competitors' offerings.

- Some categories of customers whose needs are not being met may be found. The company can follow up to satisfy their unmet needs.

- The company might learn more about the market and operation know-how by benchmarking the actions of the competitors

Research Methods of Competitor Analysis

- Internet—Read Researching on the Internet for more detail about this powerful tool.

- Personal visits—If possible, visit the competitors' locations. Observe how employees interact with customers. What do their premises look like? How are their products displayed? Priced?

- Talk to customers—The sales staff is in regular contact with customers and prospects. The competition is also in contact with these people. Learn what the customers and prospects are saying about the competitors—and about own firm, too!

- Competitors' ads—Analyze competitors' ads to gain information about their target audience, market position, product features and benefits, prices, etc.

- Speeches or presentations—Attend speeches or presentations made by representatives of the competitors.

- Trade show displays—View the competitor's display with a critical eye and from a potential customer's point of view. What does their display "say" about the company? Even observing which trade shows or industry events competitors attend provides information on their marketing strategy and target market.

- Written sources:
  General business publications
  Marketing and advertising publications
  Local newspapers and business journals
  Industry and trade association publications
  Industry research and surveys
  Computer databases (available at many public libraries)
  Annual reports
  Yellow Pages

The chapter has summarized the key measurements used in competitor analysis as follows including the key information points need to be dig into during interviews:

- Profiling
- Pricing
- Financial analysis
- Sales structure
- Human resource management
- Performance evaluation

Profiling

Definition

Profiling a company is the first preliminary step of competitor analysis which can provide a snapshot of the target company. Market researchers can make further insightful study based on the basic data and background of the target company.

The majority information in company profiling is collected by secondary research which is summarized as follows:

- Trade associations
- On-line databases
- Internet
- Syndicated market-research services
- Government agencies
- Trade press
- Newsletters
- Off-the-shelf market research reports
- Product literature
- CD-ROM
- Other published sources

However, the frequent data source market researchers normally use where they can find valuable information from is company website which can provide most information needed to outline the target company. Primary research is needed if necessary which largely depends on the depth of required insight.

Methods of Measurement

Company profiling contains all general information about the target company. The key points which should be included in company profile are illustrated as follows:

- Company General
  Company general includes company name, location, established year, employee numbers, investment amount, ownership, etc. Sometimes the ratio

between salespeople and technical staff and the ratio between export and local sales have to be provided upon request.

- Background
Company background includes growth history, information about investors which is more important to joint-venture, establishment background. For example, high-tech company must have rich establishment background. Researchers can dig further into why and how the company has been set up, what the circumstance and market situation at that time, how the company initiate the product development and production etc.

- Product
General information about product range is relatively easier to find from the company website and product catalog. However, it is more valuable to find volume share by product category in total sales revenue, the percentage of local production, local assembling, and import, function of products, points of difference in product design, production technology etc., plus after sales service strategy and new product development strategy.

- Production
Outsourced production/contract manufacturing is important information of contract production. If the company has, it is wise to know the percentage and products of outsource/contact manufactured and satisfaction in terms of speed and reliability.

- Distribution channels
Distribution channel is a interesting key point which attracts a lot of attention. Researchers are interested in how many sales offices in local market and international market, the ratio between direct sales and distributor sales, number and names of distributors etc. If the target company has strong distributors network, the further primary research can focus on distributor management such as how many distributors, how to train the distributors, how to allocate profit with distributors, how to compensate distributors, etc.

- Price
Price is a sensitive topic to the target companies if they feel the researchers are serving for their competitors. So it is wise for researchers to keep the client name confidential and don't unveil the purpose of collecting information.

The target companies are more likely to provide quotation if they feel the interviewers tend to buy their products. It is much easier to manage interviews in that way.

Price includes whole sale price and retail price, distributor price and direct sales price, etc., which should be the key points in study. Other items can not be ignored are discount and commission to distributors.

- Sales growth

  Some important measures are employed to evaluate the company growth such as revenue size, growth rate, market share. These are too sensitive for respondents to tell in the phone. Face-to-face interview is more effective way to obtain such information. Furthermore, the problem can be sorted out easily if the financial statement of the target company can be collected. Some financial research companies can provide such service such as Dun & Bradstreet. But the data of base year is not enough to see the potential and future of that company. Therefore, effective forecast method which is illustrated in Chapter 3. Market General has to be adopted here to predict the growth of the target company.

- Competitive Advantage

  The regional/national presence is the general concern which can be break up of sales by key regions. Key strengths/weaknesses/positioning in the market is the key concern to researchers from the perspectives of quality, price, niche applications etc. Keep asking the questions such as whether it is a winner/loser, whether it is a brand conscious, quality conscious player, whether it is a growth company.

- Future Plans

  Future plans can be potential business alliances, organization restructure, strategic options, key growth areas/growth potential, products, regions etc. Further question can be asked about the preferred strategy such as the respondent perception on WOFE, JV, acquisition; what are the pitfalls of alliances, risks to be aware of pose to particularly foreign companies.

Pricing

Definition

In today's marketplace, competitive pricing is important for attracting and retaining customers. Consequently, a well-planned pricing policy plays a critical role in market-oriented strategic planning.

Companies set a price for the first time when they market a new product or introduce products into a new distribution channel or geographical area. However, companies often face situations where they have to cut or raise prices. For example, prices should be decreased when there is excess plant capacity, declining market share, or recession. Likewise, prices should be increased when there is inflation or excess demand. Instead of changing prices at random, it is necessary for companies to undertake price analysis.

The goal of price analysis is to assist in the development of an effective pricing plan that indicates the appropriate price levels to use when launching a new product, and the most appropriate price levels during subsequent stages of the product life cycle.

Companies must consider different pricing strategies when selecting prices. "Pricing to penetrate" is a pricing strategy that uses a low profit margin to penetrate the market. It is designed to grab market share quickly. "Skimming the cream", on the other hand, is a strategy that uses high pricing to obtain high profits.

Markup pricing, target-return pricing, perceived-value pricing, value pricing, going-rate pricing, and sealed-bid pricing are some of the pricing strategies followed by companies. A brief explanation of these pricing methods is given below:

- Markup pricing: Companies add a standard markup to the products' cost. This is the most elementary method of pricing that companies follow.
- Target-return Pricing: Companies fix a price that would yield a target ROI.
- Perceived-value Pricing: Companies base prices on the value of the product as perceived by customers.
- Value Pricing: Companies set a low price for a high-quality offering.
- Going-rate Pricing: Companies fix prices based on competitors' prices.
- Sealed-bid Pricing: Companies adjust prices based on the expectation of how competitors will price.

Of late, the Internet has revolutionized the pricing practices followed by different companies. By using the Net, sellers can monitor customer behavior and customize product offerings. Web-based software can target shoppers for specific products and prices. At the same time, buyers can compare prices instantaneously. Price—comparison sites can help customers get a better deal. Moreover, both buyers and sellers can negotiate prices through online auctions and exchanges.

Companies cannot always depend on customers' recognizing the value of their products against that of their competitors'. So, they should continuously scan the market for prices charged by competitors. Information about prices can be gathered from the following sources:

- Product literature of competitors.
- Phone calls to the competitor's order-processing desk.
- Advertisements in magazines.
- Questioning the customers of competitors.
- Purchasing products of competitor's (a more expensive option).
- Purchasing information through market engineering services.

Since most marketing decisions are based on price, it is an extremely important parameter. Moreover, measuring price is easy as well as inexpensive. Many companies advertise their prices in the trade press. Others give their prices freely over the phone. If these methods fail, companies can approach end-users for determining prices.

It is necessary for business executives to remember that price is a dynamic variable in any market. It can sometimes be difficult to measure, especially when companies are involved in sealed—bid contracts with the government, or when discounting is prevalent. Companies should also realize that basing market strategy solely on an analysis of competitor pricing could prove detrimental, particularly if other strategic market parameters are ignored.

Methods of Measurement

Several information points can be collected during competitor interviews:

- Typical selling prices in each of the product areas
    a) Historical
    b) Current
    c) Projected
- Pricing structure (distributor margin, sales commission, customer price)
- Short term and long term pricing strategy
- Pricing Approach

    The way in which the company competes through product/service rates. This includes overall strategy, short-term tactics, general pricing process, and approach to additional charges. Attention should be given to any recent changes in pricing tactics.
- Pricing Process

    The procedures by which the company researches, prepares, bids and finalizes a pricing offer to a customer.
- Pre-Bid

    The research and information gathering process necessary to develop a price to present to the customer. Important information includes the simplicity or complexity of the pre-bid process, and the relationship between individual product pricing and total solution pricing.
- Quote/Bid Development

    The process used by the company to develop a price quote including the negotiating authority of salespeople, managers, and pricing departments; the relationship between on-the-spot pricing and "out of guideline" or pricing department pricing; the range of pricing incentives which can be offered; the amount of paperwork required of customers; the differences in developing bids for new and existing customers; variations in bid process based on customer industry or customer account segment; variations in process for bids involving multiple product lines or countries; variations in bidand the strategic planning of field salespeople in pricing. Attention should also be given to the information needed for a pricing analyst to develop a bid, including:
    - Volume?
    - Weight?
    - Cube size (dimensions)?

- Zone?
- Lane?
- Distance?
- Residential/Commercial mix (geo-type)?
- Discount for customer use of company technology?
- Competitive information?
    - Other shippers serving customer?
    - Discounts offered?
    - Revenue potential?
    - Other?
- Surcharges

    The use of charges outside of normal rates (such as currency conversion fees, fuel charges, etc.). Information would include the company's approach to these fees, the reaction of customers to these fees, the means by which the fees can be reduced or waived, salesperson authority to waive these fees.

Financial Analysis

Financial analysis is significantly important part in competitor analysis. Each company wants to have the insightful intelligence its competitors especially through its balance sheet and financial statement. Financial statement is a vital analysis tool of financial analysis. Some financial companies such as D&B is capable of providing company financial statement which can facilitate financial research much.

Here lists the key financial ratios frequently used in financial analysis. However, the primary condition to conduct successful financial research is to get the competitor's financial statement.

Current Ratio

Definition: current assets divided by current liabilities.

This ratio (sometimes called the liquidity ratio) is perhaps the best-known measure of financial strength on a specific date. The number of times current assets (cash, marketable securities, accounts, receivable, inventory) cover current liabilities (accounts and notes payable, accrued expenses, and taxes) is an important expression of the company's solvency—that is, its ability to meet obligations as they come due.

A popular rule of thumb for this ratio is two (2:1). [1] Many consider this the minimum necessary for reliable cash flow, though some lines of business (having a major portion of assets in cash) traditionally operate at lower figures. Much higher ratios could means that management is not aggressive in finding ways to put current assets to work.

Although liquidity is improved by reducing inventories and stepping up collection of receivables, this does not (by itself) alter that current ratio. It only changes the mix of the current asset accounts. The best way to solve chronic liquidity problems is to infuse new cash into the business (by borrowing or selling stock). Liquidity is usually examined monthly, or more often when the ratio is low. The year-end value may lack significance for firms experiencing large seasonal changes in activity. This ratio is traditionally expressed as a straight quotient—not a percentage.

$$CurrentRatio = \frac{CurrentAssets}{CurrentLiability} \qquad \text{(Verbal equation)}$$

Quick Ratio

Definition: Quick assets (current assets less inventory) divided by current liabilities.

This ratio (sometimes called the acid test ratio) is perhaps the best measure of liquidity on a specific date, because it deals only with those assets that can be converted to cash in a short time. The so-called quick not inventories (which are considered illiquid in the short term). This tough measure forces management to consider its ability to meet today's obligations if sales revenues should disappear, or if the business had to close its doors. A quick ratio between one-half and one (0.5:1 to 1:1) is considered satisfactory for most business if there is no reason to believe that anything will slow the collection of receivables and no negative year-to-year trends are apparent. [2].

Management has few options when dealing with a chronically-low quick ratio. Stepping up collection of receivables will improve the cash situation. Any action that increases profitability will help in the long run. The best immediate solution is to bring new money into the business.

This ratio is usually examined monthly, or more often when it is low. Because current assets and liabilities can change significantly on a daily basis, the year-end value may have little meaning. This measure also is traditionally expressed as a straight ratio—not a percentage.

$$QuickRatio = \frac{CurrentAssets - Inventory}{CurrentLiabilities}$$

Current Debt to Equity

Definition: Current liabilities divided by tangible stockholders' equity, multiplied by 100 provide a percentage.

This measure of financial strength compares what is owned currently to what is owned. Because current debt is due now, the ratio is another important indicator of solvency and receives close attention of lenders. It answers the question, "How much of the investment the owners have in their business is claimed by current debt?"

The traditional danger point for this ratio is 80%, above which ay unexpected interruption in cash flow might put the business in jeopardy. Some sources think a somewhat lower ratio of two-to-three (about 67%) is a better upper limit. [3] For small retail businesses, where most current assets are in inventory, 50% may be appropriate. [4] Replying too heavily on suppliers to provide capital is risky, and also involves loss of payment discounts. Increasing owner equity by selling more stock lowers the ratio, as does reducing current liabilities.

Intangible assets (good will, patents and trademarks, treasury stock, organization expenses) are deducted from new worth because of their illiquidity, and also because their real value is difficult to determine.

This ratio is usually examined monthly, or more often when it is high.

$$CurrentDebttoEquity = 100 \times \frac{CurrentLiabilities}{TangibleStockholders'Equity}$$

Debt to Equity

Definition: Total liabilities divided by tangible stockholders' equity, multiplied by 100 to provide a percentage.

This ratio, popular with lenders, compares the total of what is owned to what is owned. When the ratio exceeds 100%, it means that the capital provided by lenders exceeds that provided by the stockholders. Owners seeking leverage in their capitalization structure prefer a high ratio. For each dollar invested, the company is able to buy more assets, presumably leading to increased sales and a higher return to investment. Lenders, on the other hand, prefer to see a low ratio as insurance that the company is able to repay its debts.

Median values for the ratio (looking at different lines of business) vary from about 30% to more that 150%. In the case of industrial firms, many believe that values significantly above 100% require careful examination. [5] For a great many years (as a result of taxation policies which favor debt over equity), average values for this ratio have increased. Although business writers do frequently mention certain upper limits, such as 100% or even 300%, it can be argued that there really is no definitive danger point. The ability to effectively use leerage depends on the line of business, managerial skill, and luck. Managers committed to leverage might keep in mind, however, that many of the world's finest companies operate entirely without debt. [6]

Once the debt burden is undertaken, means to service it must be maintained. The higher the debt, the greater the risk that the company will find itself in trouble if sales can not be maintained at normal levels.

$$DebttoEquity = 100 \times \frac{TotalLiabilities}{TangibleStockholders'Equity}$$

Turnover of Working Capital

Definition: Net sales divided by working capital.

This ratio measures how effectively a company's working capital (current assets less current liabilities) is used to generate and process sales. When sales rise, inventories increase to match actual and anticipated orders. Payables and receivables also increase. Purchasing and credit-policy decisions must be made wisely if unexpected and serious cash shortages are to be avoided. This ratio continuously measures the complex relationship between buying and selling.

Maintaining the ratio at a low value insures availability of cash to sustain operations. But this may be an inefficient use of funds. Letting the ratio grow to a high value, on the other end, could market the company vulnerable in an adverse business climate. The best managerial goal may be to hold the ratio more-or-less constant after first determining (by experience) what works best for the company. Median values for this ratio reported by line of business vary from two or three (certain types of retailing) to 18 to more (meat packing and gas transmission).

$$TurnoverWorkingCapital = \frac{NetSales}{WorkingCapital} = \frac{Netsales}{CurrentAssets - CurrentLiabilities}$$

Supplier Financing of Assets

Definition: Accounts payable divided by total assets, multiplied by 100 to provide a percentage.

Businesses are financed in many ways, the most well-known being investor equity and long-term borrowing. Suppliers also participate in the capitalization of businesses by extending credit (usually unsecured) for the purchase of merchandise for resale. Although this is thought of as short-term credit, it is likely (if payments are kept current) to be automatically and continuously renewed.

In the case of many small- and medium-size businesses, suppliers and customers enjoy close and mutually-dependent relationships. Credit terms may be extremely generous—much better than market. The customers are, in effect, beneficiaries of interest-free, unsecured, automatically renewable lines of credit. When this type of buyer-seller relationship is identified, the financing aspects should be monitored.

There are risks in supplier financing. Despite its possible long-term character, it is short-term credit. Any number of events has potential for causing its disruption or termination. The supplier may be acquired by a larger firm unwilling to continue in the same way. The buyer may fail to meets its payment obligations and lose the special privileges. It is these questions of uncertainty that explain why supplier financing is not generally acknowledged as a source of capital.

The ratio is useful in cash flow analysis, and when questions are asked about obtaining funds to accommodate growth. When needed asset increases cannot be fully financed by profits, borrowed funds, or new equity capital, it is reasonable to ask if supplier financing might possibly make up the difference.

Credit extended by sellers in the form of open accounts also shows up in the ratio Current Debt to Equity.

If accounts payable fluctuates significantly during the year, the calculation may have little meaning on a particular date. In that case it is better to use an average figure in the numerator.

$$SupplierFinancing of Assets = 100 \times \frac{Accounts Payable}{Total Assets}$$

Cash to Total Liabilities

Definition: Cash divided by total liabilities, multiplied by 100 to provide a percentage.

Cash ratios are not very popular. One reason is for this is that a company's money position varies dramatically from day to day. Many managers object ot being examined on matters that are short-term in nature, and where various strategies are available ot deal with each problem. Another reason is the belief that inventories and receivables are always there to be converted to cash when management desires. Although these observations are correct, cash ratios are nevertheless important because cash is the ultimate assets.

When W.T.Gran filed for bankruptcy in 1975, its working capital figures appeared satisfactory. What the figures did not show was the low quality of accounts receivable and a very serious shotage of cash. [7] Even if inventories are not overstated and receivables are fully collectible, time to convert them may be insufficient to meet credit demand. Cash is cash.

Critics of this ratio might say that measuring cash to total liabilities makes no sense because only part of the long-term debt is due now. If viewed in terms of coverage, this is true. If viewed as an indicator of immediate liquidity relative to the company's size, howver, total debt is a sensible measuring base.

Comparative information on levels of cash held by corporations is not easily obtained. Breakdowns of working capital can sometimes be found in annual reports in sections called, "Management Discussion and Analysis."

If marketable securities can be liquidated within a few days, they are included in numerator.

$$CashtoTotalLiabilities = 100 \times \frac{Cash}{TotalLiabilities} = 100 \times \frac{Cash}{CurrentLiabilities + LongtermLiabilities}$$

Cash to Disbursements

Definition: Cash divided by average monthly disbursements, multiplied by 100 to provide a percentage.

Just as a family compares the balance in its checking account to its habitual level of spending, companies need to look at cash positions relative to expenditures. If cash falls below a certain level, important purchases may have to be postponed and payments to creditors delayed.

This ratio is useful in preparing cash-flow budgets. After expenditures are project ed for a future period, historical values for the ratio are used to estimate the amount of cash likely to be needed in the forthcoming period. If the cash-flow budget indicates a likely insufficiency, plans can be made to correct the situation. Cash can be increased by improving management of receivables and inventory, soliciting more cash and credit card sales relative to open account sales, obtaining or increasing a bank line of credit, slowing payments to suppliers, selling company stock, and so forth.

The denominator, average monthly disbursements, is formed by adding the year's total expenses to the year's purchases, and then dividing the sum by 12. By using a monthly base, a manager is provided with figure representing a percentage of one month's average cash outlay. Thus if average monthly expenditures are $ 157,000 and cash on hand is $46,000, the cash to disbursements ratio is 29.3%.

The ratio can also be used to express coverage of a certain number of day's expenditures by multiplying the result by 21, which in the above example is about six business days. Of course, in most circumstances cash will also be coming in during the month. The ratio calculated in days, therefore, represents the lower limit of realistic coverage.

As with all ratios involving cash, the result of computation varies markedly from day to day as payments are made to suppliers and funds are received from customers. For some uses of the ratio, average cash values are more meaningful in numerator than values at year end.

$$CashtoDisbursements = 100 \times \frac{Cash}{AverageMonthlyDisbursements} = 100 \times \frac{Cash}{\frac{TotalExpense + Purchase}{12}}$$

Sales Structure

Definition

Sales Structure is the way in which the company organizes people and functions to sell to customers. This includes position/job titles, number of people fulfilling each function, geography- and industry-based organization (for example: automotive industry sales team, fashion industry sales team), specialized sales forces by product or company business, and specialized sales forces for small, new, growing, and existing customers.

Sales force are usually assigned geographic areas. However, fewer organizations are expecting to be focused on all customers within a geographic area without further specialization. For a smart competitive intelligence researcher, he must dig into the detailed breakup of sales force to understand the advantage and possible pitfalls of such structure.

The most common types of sales force specializations are geographic, product, customer and functional specializations as follows:

Chart 4.1 Sales Structure: Geographic Specialized Sales Force

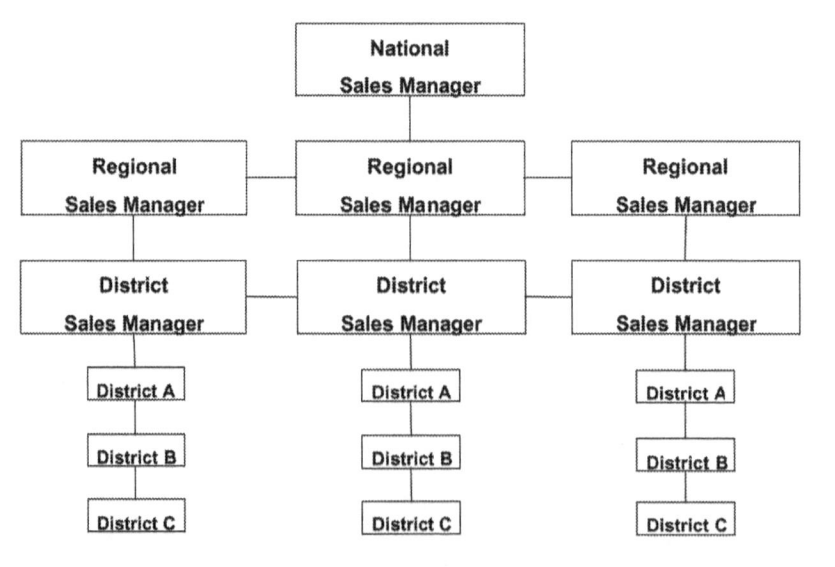

An important advantage of changing from a completely open sales force structure to geographic specialization is that travel time and expenses are reduced. Customer service may also improve because the number of customers to be serviced is limited a and geographically concentrated. The diagram also minimized conflict over who is responsible for getting the job done in each area. A geographic organization works best when the product line consists of related products or series that appeal to rather homogenous group of buyers [8].

Chart 4.2 Sales Structure: Product Specialized Sales Force

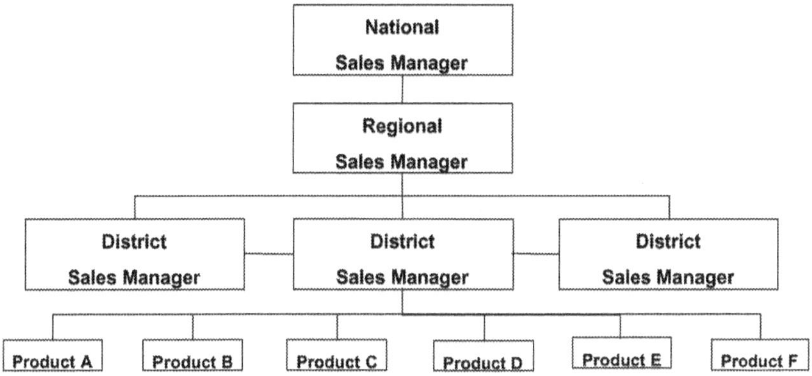

```
                    ┌─────────────────┐
                    │    National     │
                    │  Sales Manager  │
                    └────────┬────────┘
                    ┌────────┴────────┐
                    │    Regional     │
                    │  Sales Manager  │
                    └────────┬────────┘
        ┌────────────────────┼────────────────────┐
   ┌────┴─────┐        ┌─────┴────┐         ┌─────┴────┐
   │ District │        │ District │         │ District │
   │  Sales   │        │  Sales   │         │  Sales   │
   │ Manager  │        │ Manager  │         │ Manager  │
   └──┬───┬───┘        └──┬───┬───┘         └──┬───┬───┘
  ┌───┴┐ ┌┴───┐      ┌───┴┐ ┌┴────┐      ┌────┴┐ ┌┴────┐
  │Prod│ │Prod│      │Prod│ │Prod │      │Prod │ │Prod │
  │ A  │ │ B  │      │ C  │ │ D   │      │ E   │ │ F   │
  └────┘ └────┘      └────┘ └─────┘      └─────┘ └─────┘
```

Companies may switch to product specialization for one of several reasons. For instance, salespersons may need greater knowledge to sell technologically complex product lines. Another common reason is because new products may be added (either through new product development or acquiring another company), which are quite different from existing product lines or are sold to a different customer segment [9].

Chart 4.3 Sales structure: Customer Specialization Sales Force

```
                          ┌─────────────────┐
                          │    National     │
                          │  Sales Manager  │
                          └────────┬────────┘
        ┌──────────────────────────┼──────────────────────────┐
┌───────────────┐          ┌───────────────┐          ┌───────────────┐
│   Regional    │          │   Regional    │          │   Regional    │
│ Sales Manager │          │ Sales Manager │          │ Sales Manager │
└───────┬───────┘          └───────┬───────┘          └───────┬───────┘
┌───────────────┐          ┌───────────────┐          ┌───────────────┐
│   District    │          │   District    │          │   District    │
│ Sales Manager │          │ Sales Manager │          │ Sales Manager │
└───────────────┘          └───────────────┘          └───────────────┘
┌──────────────┬──────────────┬──────────────┬──────────────┐
│Salesperson for│Salesperson for│Salesperson for│Salesperson for│
│Customer Group A│Customer Group B│Customer Group C│Customer Group D│
└──────────────┴──────────────┴──────────────┴──────────────┘
```

Product specialization allows salespeople to become experts in a particular product line and selling process, this type of organization likely to be more expensive than a simple geographic organization.

A customer focused organizational structure is more market driven. Salespeople must be well supported to be customer experts and industry specialists. Such structure can help to better spot selling opportunities and to increase customer satisfaction.

Chart 4.4 Sales Structure: Functional Specialization of Sales Structure

A fourth type of specialization in sales organization, functional specialization focuses on the jobs or function performed by customer contract people.

These four types of specialization have been fully adopted into the sales force hierarchy by most multinational companies (MNC) with growing globalization. The concept of cross-linked sales structure can be illustrated in Chart 4.5.

Chart 4.5 Sales Structure: Cross-linked Sales Structure

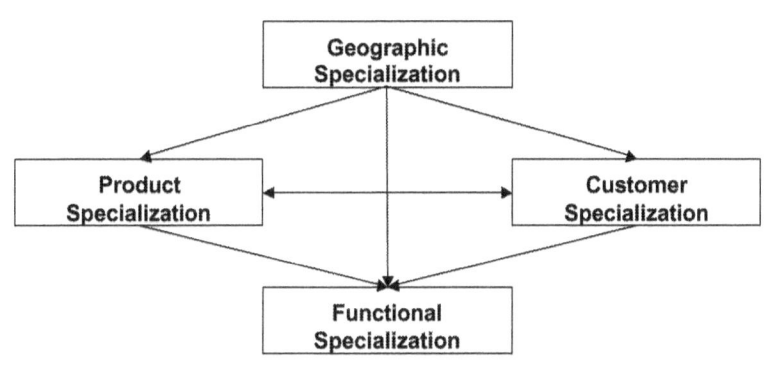

General speaking, toping the sales structure of most MNC is the regional sales office which is the first layer of sales structure and defined by geographic specialization. In each sales region, the sales force is separated by product or customer specialization. The functional specialization structure may be identified in some companies e.g. Gillette, Fedex. These classifications are the second layer of sales structure. There may exist the third layer in sales structure for some industrial giants. In each product (customer) category, the sales force may be divided by another customer (product) specialization or functional specialization.

Methods of Measurement

In perception of sales structure of competitors, following questions can be developed to catch more detailed information from primary research:

- Number of sales offices and geographic coverage
- Number of sales staff/organization/expertise

- How does the company organize its sales force
- Any planned changes to these arrangements.

Customer Specialization:

- Which parts of the sales structure are responsible for which groups of customers
- How the company categorizes customer accounts
- What positions within the sales force are responsible for each group of customer
- How, when, and why that responsibility is transferred between salespeople

Product specialization:

- Which parts of the sales structure are responsible for which product
- How the company categorizes product
- How, when, and why that responsibility is transferred between salespeople

Functional/Geographic specialization:

- Which business units maintain their own sales forces and which rely on a central sales force
- The ways is the sales force is related to the rest of the company
- The ways in which one sales force is related to another
- The connections in organization and personnel between Asia & Europe, Asia & the US, and Europe & the US.

Human Resource Management

Human resource management contains the policies and practices by which the company creates, maintains and operates its sales organization such as recruiting criteria, career development, training etc.

Recruiting

Recruiting is the strategies the company uses to attract and evaluate new salespeople and sales management which includes the qualifications sought in sales personnel i.e. industry knowledge, knowledge of area, sales background, education, the image the company presents to potential recruits, and the techniques the company uses to identify potential recruits etc. Also, whether previous or current employees of other competitors are sought after or avoided.

Some sorts of specific questions as follows can be asked in primary research with competitors:

■ How do you decide on the number of sales persons?

The number of new salespeople needed will depend on several factors, including sales growth targets, distribution strategies, changes in sales force organization, and sales force turnover. Nevertheless, some companies decide this number in terms of sales region distribution. For example, FedEx decide the number of salespeople according to the number of postcode since its sales force is divided by sales region and each salesperson takes care of the sales in one postcode area.

■ How do you attract a large number of qualified candidates?

There are many ways to attract more job seeker's attention. Some companies emphasize on the competitive salary and welfare allowance package; others may choose to stress on the opportunities to access to cutting-edge technology which can offer employees good working experience. In comparison, salary attractiveness is more effective in practice. Some other attractivenesses are often used. For example, multinational companies usually highlight company history, background, and high reputation.

■ What is your job description?

Generally, job description includes (1) specific tasks to be carried out (2) how employee interacts with stuff in other department (3) the customers to be called on (4) mental and physical demands (5) the type of products to be touched [1].

■ What is your job qualification?

Job qualifications refer to the aptitudes, skills, knowledge, and personality traits necessary to perform the job successfully. A statement of job qualifications would typically include education, previous working experience, technical expertise, aptitudes, and interests. There is a increasing trend in recent years, companies tend to screen the candidates by personalities in the first selection step who prefer to choose the people more fit to the company culture and working atmosphere. Typical of many other companies, FedEx implements human based recruiting policy to find the right persons who are the most qualified to work in express service industry. It has four indispensable personality requirements: (1) virtuous, ingenuous, and upright (2) open and international (3) optimistic and active (4) team working spirit. Certainly, it has other requirements for different post applicants such as, the management experience for manger, the professional qualification and skills for tech staff, etc. The requirements for junior position i.e. couriers are college diploma, driving license, basic English on communication level. But the most important is still applicant's personality must be competent to work in the service industry.

For market researchers, further questions can be asked are why and how the respondent's company comes to such qualifications. This is more important than simply asking what the qualifications you use are.

■ Where do you advertise your job recruitment?

Classified advertisement in newspaper and trade journals are often used to attract salespeople. However, the best way to attract job seekers is to advertise on the professional job market which can be job newspaper, job website, etc.

■ Do you target competitors' employees or present internal employees?

Present employees often make good candidates, because they are familiar with the company's products and procedures and do not require as much training as prospects recruited from outside sources. Competitor's employee sometimes can make more profits for company if they can bring existing customers to the new company which usually happens in market research and consulting industries, sometimes in pharmaceutical industry.

Further questions can be asked is what pros and cons are and how to recruit competitor's employees. The picture of recruiting competitor's employees in the specific industry can be made by this question.

■ Do you outsource recruitment to employment agencies?

Employment agencies are a frequently used source of candidates. Generally, in China, especially for the multinational companies, they would like to outsource recruitments to the job agencies, so-called "Hunter", for some positions which they feel hard to find well-qualified candidates because of the high requirements of professional skills and knowledge or other senior positions which needs rich experience in high management level.

To market researchers in this case, it will be better to ask for what reasons the company choose "Hunters" to understand which important position the competitor needs urgently and what essential qualification needed for this position.

■ How do you perform school and colleges employment?

College candidates always are an attractive source of candidates for a number of reasons. Graduates tend to be more easily trained and are often more poised and mature than those without college training. In China, most attractive companies to college graduates are multinational companies, because of the competitive salary package, comfortable working condition and much knowledgeable and informative training programs etc. For some multinational companies with high reputation, they all have college recruitment plan each year or biannually.

Some specific questions can be asked in primary research are how often the college recruitment will be conducted, which position opened to college graduates, what type of training offered to fresh graduates, how long the probation is, etc.

■ Can you elaborate on the selection process?

Managers are responsible for the screening of a pool of candidates. The unique and preliminary approach is interview. Usually there are several round various types of interviews waiting for each applicants.

It is incumbent to a market consultant to look into the interview methods are adopted and why, such as face-to-face, telephone, one-to-one, group, team work, etc., how many round of interviews, what the major task of each round of interview is, who is present in each round of interview, what the usually asked questions are, what the hiring criteria is, etc.

■ How do you conduct background and credit checks?

Some companies have credit check process to assess candidates learning and working capability. Such check has many test approaches such as intelligence test, personality test, aptitude test, etc. Most of these credit tests are conducted in written paper.

Advancement/Career Development

Career development is the policies and practices related to employees' career growth. Whether the manaeger is recruited from outside the company or promoted from the ranks of junior level empolyee, the ways in which an employee might take on greater responsibility, the availability of opportunities within the company for employees, and the ways in which employees change jobs within the organization so-called career path.

Some specific questions can be asked as follows:

■ What are the promotion requirements? How do you evaluate promotion candidates?
■ Is there any working time requirement for any senior position?
■ Is there job transfer between departments? How to performance if yes?
■ What is the job description and job qualification difference between senior position and junior position?
■ Can you elaborate the difference in compensation and benefits after promotion?

Training

Training is the strategies, policies and procedures the company uses to educate and improve the skills of salespeople. Particular attention should be paid to the style of training i.e. formal, informal, on-the-job training (OJT), mentoring, etc., the location of training such as local or central, responsibilities of management in the training process, how often training is given, the differences between ongoing training and training for new salespeople, and which part of the corporate organization is responsible for providing, monitoring and evaluating training.

Some specific questions can be asked in research in training strategies:

- Can you talk about your company's training budget? How do you come to it? Normally, the training time and training budget is different from new employee to veteran employee. Some companies would like to spend more time on new employee but not more money. For example, FedEx offers $2,500 training allowance to each employee including new junior employee and veteran senior manager.

 More attention should be taken is why and how the company comes to this budget and further understand the difference of training offered to new employees and veteran employees.

- What are the topics in training programs? Training topics usually includes products knowledge, sale process and tactics, improving teamwork, customer and market information, company orientation, etc.

- Where to train the employees? Training can be centralized, decentralized. Either style has its own positive and negative effects shown in Figure 4.1.

Figure 4.1 Human Resource Management: Training Styles

Style	Positive	Negative
Centralized	Quality and consistency	Costly and time consuming
Decentralized	Closer to the customers and directly involves field sales management	Content and quality vary widely across the branches.

Most companies take two styles together to make up the pitfalls. For example, FedEx offers all salespeople regional training program. Meanwhile, it chooses one city in Asia Pacific region to conduct centralized training sessions for all salespeople in Asia Pacific areas twice each year to let all sales-people in different offices to meet together to share their sales tactics and skills.

In this case, research focus can be the various types of training offered, what the characteristics of each type is, what each type of training can offer, which type of training employees prefer, etc.

■ Which types of training media are employed?
Numerous media can be adopted in training such as Role-playing, games and simulations, audiotapes, emerging technology-based training methods, etc. The market researchers should dig into what the purpose of each type of media is and what the most effective media is, etc.

■ Which types of training media are employed?
The three most popular types of trainers are regular line executives, staff personnel, and outside specialists. Because each has certain advantages, it is not unusual to find organizations using all three types. The selection of trainers for individual firms depends on where the sessions are held, the size of the firm, the characteristics of the product line, and the focus of the training [10]. Obviously, the reasons for selection of trainers are market consultants' focus.

■ How do you evaluate the training?
In world perspective, most companies even reputable multinational companies do not have training evaluation system which reduces the pressure to trainees extensively, however, discounts the training quality at the same time. Market researchers may probe whether the company has training evaluation and how does it perform.

Compensation

Compensation is the pay schedule for salespeople. Compensation is one of the most important tools for motivating and retaining field salespeople. However, compensation is a cost, and selling expenses have now increased to the point where they represent 10.0 percent of sales revenue [11].

A research consultant must be able to identify the competitors' various components of the pay schedule including base/fixed pay, commission/performance measurement related pay, vehicle allowance including type of vehicle, expense account, daily allowance, expenses reimbursed by company, profit sharing and any other components of pay such as shopping trips, etc., as well as the differences for specialized sales forces. Also, the degree of flexibility in the compensation system, including typical adjustments to compensation plans, authority for making adjustments, and reasons for making adjustments, especially changes not connected to performance measurements or sales behaviors.

There are variability in compensation structure which can be illustrated in Chart 4.6.

Variable measurement is the relationship between compensation and performance including the links between compensation, performance measurement and company business strategy which contains the limits (ceiling) of variable compensation, whether the variable component adds to or subtracts from salesperson pay and the attractiveness of the program to top salespeople.

Chart 4.6 Human Resource Management: Variable Compensation

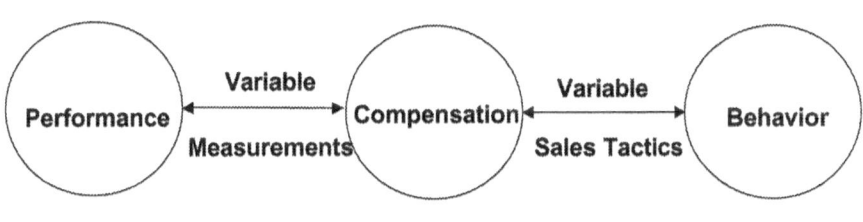

Variable sales tactics is the relationship between compensation and the behavior of salespeople. Attention should be given to the way in which the compensation program focuses salesperson attention and activity on:

- inbound, outbound, and payer business
- new customers, growing customers and existing customers

- products or services
- long-term company objectives
- short-term company objectives
- coordinated sales activity
- sales across business units
- sales with third-party organizations
- company profitability and/or yield component

Performance Evaluation

Performance evaluation/measurement means by which salesperson effectiveness is evaluated, including the points of measurement used by the company, variations of measurements specific to a country or area, business unit, and salesperson job including the policies and procedures for adjusting these performance goals based on addition or deletion of customer accounts from a salesperson's responsibility, changes in company business plan, or large-scale event such as a natural disaster.

A great unresolved controversy in sales management is whether output measures, shown in Fig. 4.2, input factors such as those in Fig 4.3, or qualitative criteria are best/or evaluating sales performance. Output factors look at sales volume, number of new accounts, margins, and the number of orders, whereas input criteria measure expenses, number of calls and days worked [1].

Some companies extensively implements input factor evaluation. For instance, FedEx has 2 sales division: telephone sales and face-to-face sales. There are some typical input valuation factors in internal sales performance assessment. The telephone salespersons are required to make 30 phone calls everyday. Likewise, the face-to-face salespersons are required to visit 5 customers every day and must stay with each customer for at least 4 hours. These are innegotiatable evaluation standards in FedEx.

Qualitative measures include attitude, communication skills, and product knowledge. Research has shown that qualitative factors are the most widely used, but they are difficult to measure and often lead to biased evaluation [12].

Figure 4.2 Performance Evaluation: Output Measures

Measures	Factors
Sales	Sales volume/ revenues
	Sales volume by product/customer
	Historic sales record
	Sales to quota
	Sales growth
	New account sales
	Sales volume to potential
Accounts	Number of new accounts
	Number of account lost
	Number of account buying full line
Profit	Net profit
	Gross margin percentage/value
	Return on investment
	Profit growth
	Margin by product
Order	Number of orders
	Average size of orders

Figure 4.3 Performance Evaluation: Input/Behaviour Measures

Measures
Selling expenses to budget
Total expenses
Selling expenses percentage of sales
Number of calls
Number of calls per day
Number of reports turned in
Number of days worked
Selling time vs. nonselling time

Figure 4.4 Performance Evaluation: Qualitative Measures

Measures
Communication skills
Product knowledge
Attitude
Selling skills
Initiative and aggressiveness
Appearance and manner
Knowledge of competition
Team player
Enthusiasm
Time management
Cooperation
Judgment
Motivation
Ethical/Moral behaviour
Planning ability
Pricing knowledge
Report preparation and submission
Creativity

In competitive research, attention should also be given to measurements of company technology use by customers such as bar codes, shipping systems, web site, measurements based on inbound such as consignee or receiver volume, and measurements which are not linked to compensation. Also important are the process and authority for setting revenue goals and the frequency with which these goals change.

Certain performance measurements are very common throughout the industry and should be given extra attention. For these, please identify the actual expectation of company of salespeople and sales management, for instance, what level is to be achieved as well as the level usually achieved.

Some key specific questions as follows can be asked in interview with salespersons:

- Any special requirement for the amount of time spent with customer
- How about the requirement of number/volume of customer contacts per day
- Is there any restriction on time spent on non-sales activity
- What is the expected customer shipping volume or revenue generated from customer
- Any requirement on time spent on new customers, growing customers, and current customers
- How is the profit measurement
- Other (as identified during interview)

Notes and References

[1] Jack Zwick, A Handbook of Small Business Finance, Small Business Management Series No. 15 (Washington, DC: Small Business Administration, 1975), p. 19

[2] John Downes and Jordan Elliot Goodman, Barron's Finance & Investment Handbook (Hauppauge, NY: Barron's Educational Series, 1990), p. 91

[3] Dun & Bradstreet, Industry Norms and Key Business Ratios, Desk Top Edition, 1990-91 (Murray Hill, NJ: 1991), p.v.

[4] Rischard Sanzo, Ratio Analysis for Small Business, Small Business Management Series No. 20 (Washington,DC: Small Business Administration, 1977), p.59

[5] Downes and Goodman, p.92

[6] Using Value Line's Value/Screen II investment software system and a database of 1,606 widely traded companies, a study by the author in 1991 found more than 6% of these companies to be entirely free of long-term debt.

[7] Harlan D. Platt, Why Companies Fail (Lexington, MA: Heath, 1985), p. 34-35

[8] Robert Ruekert, Orville walker, and Kenneth Roering, "The organization of Marketing Activities: A Contingency Theory of Structure and Performance," Journal of Marketing, 49 (Winter 1985), pp. 17-21

[9] Martin Everett, "Send in the specialists", Sales & Marketing Management (April 1991), pp. 46-47

[10] Douglas J. Dalrymple, William L. Cron, Thomas E. Decarlo, "Sales Management (7th Ed.)" John Wiley & Sons, Inc. (2001)

[11] Sales Force Compensation Survey (Chicago: Dartmell Corporation, 1999), p. 117.

[12] Donald, W.Jackson, John L. Schlacter, and William G. Wolfe, "Examing the Bases Utilized for Evaluating Salespeoples' performance", Journal of Personal Selling & Sales Management, Vol. 15, No. 4 (Fall 1995), P.64.

Chapter 5

Consumer Analysis

The american marketing association: defines market research as: "The systematic gathering, recording, and analysis of data about problems relating to the marketing of goods and services". Consumer analysis is an important part of this marketing research.

Consumer analysis is a study of relevant psychological, sociological, and anthropological variables that shape intentions, activities, and motivations of those in the exchange process which focus on both the individual and social influence determinants of buying and consuming behaviors. Individual, family, and group buying decision processes is widely examined.

Consumer behavior is a dynamic, exciting field whose study is the consumer. And it is knowledge and understanding of the consumer that enables marketing managers to plan effective marketing strategies, to generate satisfactory product designs, to communicate clearly with target markets, and to enhance consumer quality of life.

This chapter will cover various measurements as follows:

- Segmentation
- Awareness, attitude & usage (AAU)
- Concept
- Customer satisfaction
- Customer loyalty
- Brand image

- Brand equity
- Pricing
- Advertising

Segmentation

Market segmentation identifies and targets the groups of customers most likely to purchase the products and services being offered.

Customers are grouped using a variety of techniques and descriptors. Traditionally market segments are identified using characteristics such as demographics, psychographics, behavioral activities, technical knowledge, different usage and purchase situations, benefits sought from the product, usage rates, and even geographic area.

The purpose of market segmentation is to classify groups of customers by product usage rates, or the likelihood of purchasing the product or service in the future. However, simple identification of these groups does not guarantee that this information is meaningful in a business sense. Effective segmentation places requirements on the market. The market segment must be as follows:

- Measurable

  The market segment must be measurable. We must be able to identify segmentation variables that are related to purchase of the product and develop a descriptive profile of the market segment using a combination of variables.

- Accessible

  The market segment must be accessible. That is, in addition to being able to identify the market segment we must be able to reach them in an efficient and cost-effective manner. Do they belonged to specific chat groups, newsgroups, or subscribe to online publications? Perhaps they subscribe to one or more computer magazines, or have purchased from a specific catalog.

- Substantial

  The market segment must have the ability to purchase. Almost all college seniors want to have a new Porsche or Corvette, but few have the ability to purchase such an expensive two seat sports car.

- Actionable

  The market segment must produce the differential response when exposed to the market offering. That is, they must be willing to purchase

Which method market segmentation is most effective? Of course it depends on the specific product or service being considered. The preparation of content for advertisements or Web pages would rely heavily on benefit segmentation. The design of an economical automobile for a young single woman would of course rely heavily on demographics as well as psychographics.

Many market segmentation studies focus on understanding the tangible and intangible meanings attached to a product or service, or providing a descriptive analysis of past, current or potential purchasers of the product.

Product Attributes:

- Country Ties—Geographic area, country of origin
- Competitive Analysis
- Product Class Perceptions
- Life Style—Personality—Psychographics
- Product identity: celebrity identity, personality
- User—Customer demographics
- Use Occasion—Application
- Relative Price Comparisons and Sensitivity
- Customer Benefits
- Intangibles

These areas can be further broken down into several categories:

1. What are the external characteristics of the segment?
   - Demographic
   - Geographic
   - Family Life Cycle

2. Do they have the ability to buy?
   - Socioeconomic

3. What are the internal characteristics of the segment?
   - Culture
   - Personality

- Self-concept
- Psychographics
- Activities, Interests, Opinions

4. What do the segments like and dislike?
   - Awareness
   - Attitudes

5. What product or service attributes made a difference in their purchase?
   - Attitudes
   - Beliefs
   - Benefits
   - Motivation
   - Involvement
   - Values
   - Satisfaction

6. How do members of each segment make decisions or behave?
   - Situational decision making
   - Decision making style
   - Information processing style

7. How do members of the segment intend to behave?
   - Intention to purchase

8. How have they acted in specific situations in the past?
   - Past purchases
   - Brand loyalty
   - Information search and evaluation
   - Decision-attribute tradeoffs

One practical example of segementation identification is shown in Chart 5.1

Chart 5.1 Segmentation: Segmentation identification

TASTE

Size: 30%
Behavior: Spearmint lovers
Psychographics: High selfinvolvement
Demographics: Children

COSMETIC

Size: 20%
Behavior: Smokers
Psychographics: Highsociabilities
Demographics: Teens, young adults

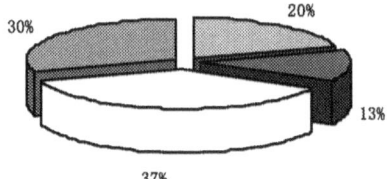

ECONOMY

Size: 37%
Behavior: Heavy users
Psychographics: High autonomy, value oriented
Demographics: Men

MEDICAL COSMETIC TESTE

Size: 13%
Behavior: Heavy users
Psychographics: Hypochondria
Demographics: Large families

Most market segmentation studies use variants of standard segmentation questions. The combination of question purpose, approach, and format for question and response creates an endless set of options to be considered when designing a market segmentation questionnaire.

A variety of concepts, such as demographics, are commonly measured in many market studies. If you were to examine some of the customer satisfaction questionnaires to which you have been asked to respond, you would find that many contain the same concepts. You would also observe that many questions have minor variations in the response scales used.

One important key to maximizing the effectiveness of survey research and measurement is to establish and maintain comparable response scales. This comparability, if present, is useful in linking the current study to previous research, be it of primary or secondary source. For example, in the United States, researchers often match demographic scales with those of the Census of Population. Other applications may require standards that are industry or company based. The point being that comparability between data sources and study results is much easier when scales are similar.

Awareness, Attitude and Usage (AAU)

One of the most basic, exploratory forms of marketing research is the AUA (Awareness, Attitude and Usage) This type of survey is used to assess the general state of the market for a particular brand, product, or service. These surveys can draw on the opinions of both consumer and/or business customers.

■ Awareness

Awareness is the extent to which a brand name is recalled as a member of a brand, product or service class, as distinct from brand recognition.

Common market research usage is that pure brand awareness requires "unaided recall". For example a respondent may be asked to recall the names of any cars he may know, or any whisky brands he may know.

Some researchers divide awareness into both "unaided" and "aided" recall. "Aided recall" measures the extent to which a brand name is remembered when the actual brand name is prompted. An example of such a question is "Do you know of the "Honda" brand?"

In terms of brand exposure, companies want to look for high levels of unaided recall in relation to their competitors. The first recalled brand name (often called "top of mind") has a distinct competitive advantage in brand space, as it has the first chance of evaluation for purchase.

Similar to brand awareness, Ad awareness can also be categorized into three recall categories including top-of-mind, spontaneous, prompted.

■ Attitude

Attitudes are the opinions associated with the brands, products, etc. that are being tested. The attitudes towards the brands can help determine strengths or "equities" (which should be preserved) and weaknesses (that should be corrected.)

brand awareness is an essential ingredient in the consideration set of potential purchases. Brand awareness is particularly important in markets where consumers make top-of-mind buying decisions. In such markets, consumers often make decisions based on the image of the brand that comes to mind automatically.

■ Usage

Usage patterns, which are a subset of the demographic profile, help reveal the how the respondents are interacting with the brand, product or service. This is particularly important as a comparative measurement against the attitudes—e.g. Do heavy users have different opinions or priorities than the occasional users? Other demographics, such as gender, age, income, etc. also help to isolate particular groups that are particularly good (or bad) prospective customers.

Usage can be categorized into 2 categories: brand usage, brand purchase, and unmet needs. Brand usage includes ever used, conversion, and preference. Brand purchase includes key buying factors (KBF)s, frequency, volume, spending, and channel.

Concept

The concept testing is perceived as how people, without prompting, interpret deliberately a sketchy idea for a new product or service [2].

Concept testing is most often used in concept development to test the success of a new product idea before it is marketed. Concept analysis or concepts are often used as one step in the process of providing "proof of concept".

Potential consumers are involved to provide their reactions to written statements, images or graphics, or actual implementations of the basic idea for the product. Concept testing is most often a GO/No Go screening that serves to kill those concepts that have very little potential.

Concept testing and development provides the direction and guidance necessary to selectively identify and communicate key product or service benefits, uses, packaging, advertising, sales approaches, product information, distribution, and pricing.

Reaction of Potential Customers

The reactions of potential customers can be tested at several stages of the creative development cycle. When the idea is young, it can be tested as a "concept statement" which is a succinct paragraph describing the key messages. As the idea proceeds to actual renderings, various options can be tested to see which one produces the best results. It is often desirable to test the various underlying messages' appeal to make sure that the messages themselves are on target (e.g. you can have an ad which communicates unimportant messages very well.)

Getting customer feedback for the development of new products is a vital role of marketing research. In general, there are three distinct phases of new product development in which research can be useful: 1) Determining market requirements, 2) Testing features and design alternatives and 3) Measuring aspects of market feedback related to commercialization.

Determining the market requirements involves determining the gaps between what is currently available and what customers' ultimately desire. In addition, market requirements research attempts to determine how much better a new product must be in order to be perceived as "good enough to switch." Finally, this stage of research can be used to determine overall reactions to a new product concept and get a preliminary read on market potential for the product or service.

During the design phase of the product or service, frequent iterations of testing with potential customers can provide valuable feedback to the design team. Feature testing, in-home studies and focus groups can be used to answer questions from the consumers' standpoint.

Concept Test

The purpose of concept test is measure which product/brands are more acceptable to the public. The basic methodology can be summarized into 2 categories:

- Qualitative

  Qualitative measurement can make various sketchy ideas converge into several concepts. It can unveil in-depth reasons behind and calibrate the concept which is more suitable to perceive different benefits of single product. The shortage of the qualitative method is limited number of screening concepts and no data support.

- Quantitative

  The quantitative research process can be summarized as follows:
  1) The product concepts are categorized into 3 stacks: interested in purchasing, not interested in purchasing, and uncertain.
  2) Choose 3 concept cards from the interested in purchasing group and ask about the key message, uniqueness, and believability.
  3) Choose 2 concept cards from the not interested in purchasing group and ask about the dislikes.

The basic measurement factors can be: easy to understand, uniqueness, believability, overall liking, likes vs. dislikes, purchase intent, improvement, imagery, price/value for money etc.

Customer Satisfaction

Customer satisfaction is "the state of mind that customers have about a company and its products or services when their expectations have been met or exceeded. This state reflects the lifetime of the product or service experience."

The best approach to measuring customer satisfaction and building customer satisfaction surveys depends on the kind of product or service provided, the kinds of customers served, how many customers are served, the longevity and frequency of customer/supplier interactions, and what you intend to do with the results.

Three very different approaches both produce meaningful and useful findings:

- Post Purchase Evaluation
  Satisfaction feedback is obtained from the individual customer at the time of product or service delivery (or shortly afterwards). This type of satisfaction survey is typically used as part of a CRM (Customer Relationship Management System) and focuses on having a long term relationship with the individual customer

- Periodic Satisfaction Surveys
  Satisfaction feedback from groups of customers at periodic intervals to provide an occasional snapshot of customer experiences and expectations.

- Continuous Satisfaction Tracking
  Satisfaction feedback is obtained from the individual customer at the time of product or service delivery (or shortly afterwards). Satisfaction tracking surveys are often part of a management initiative to assure quality is at high levels over time.

Satisfaction surveys are developed to provide an understanding of customers' expectations and satisfaction. Satisfaction surveys typically require multiple questions that address different dimensions of the satisfaction concept. Satisfaction measurement includes measures of overall satisfaction, satisfaction with individual product and service attributes, and satisfaction with the benefits of purchase. Satisfaction measurement is like peeling away layers of an onion-each layer reveals yet another deeper layer, closer to the core.

All three methods of conducting satisfaction surveys are helpful methods to obtain customer feedback for assessing overall accomplishments, degree of success, and areas for improvement.

Customer satisfaction usually leads to customer loyalty and product repurchase. But measuring satisfaction is not measuring loyalty. The following are typical satisfaction questions asked:

- Importance—the importance of service/product in each specific aspect.
- Satisfaction—How is the customer satisfaction? Compared with competitors' satisfaction.
- Priority—the vital aspects need to take further step to improve.

These satisfaction survey questions can be asked in a number of different ways, focusing on different reference points focus on:

- Expectations and their Confirmation or Disconfirmation (was worse, better than expected)
- Performance of the product or service
- Emotional measures of satisfaction (good feelings, bad feelings, happy, sad)
- Willingness to repeat behavior (assumes satisfaction)
- Direct measures of overall satisfaction

In addition, the scales used in customer satisfaction surveys vary from a simple 5 point "Very Satisfied to Not at all Satisfied" scale to graphical scales targeted at special groups such as children (smiling faces scale).

Some of these satisfaction scales are demonstrated in the Chart 5.2-5.4 Note that there are many, many variations of each of these scales, that might reflect slight wording changes or different numbers of scale items.

Chart 5.2 Customer Satisfaction: Claimed Importance

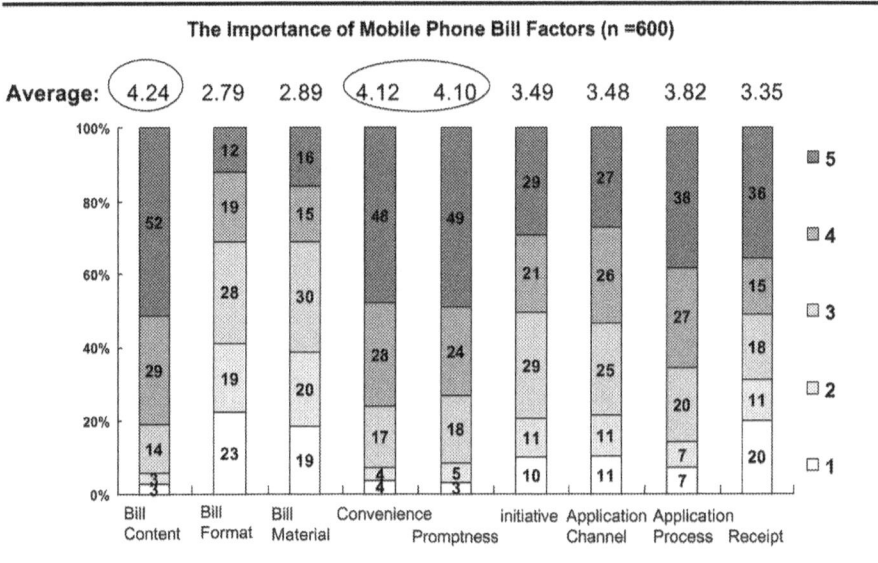

Note: *All figures are rounded.*

Chart 5.3 Customer Satisfaction: Performance

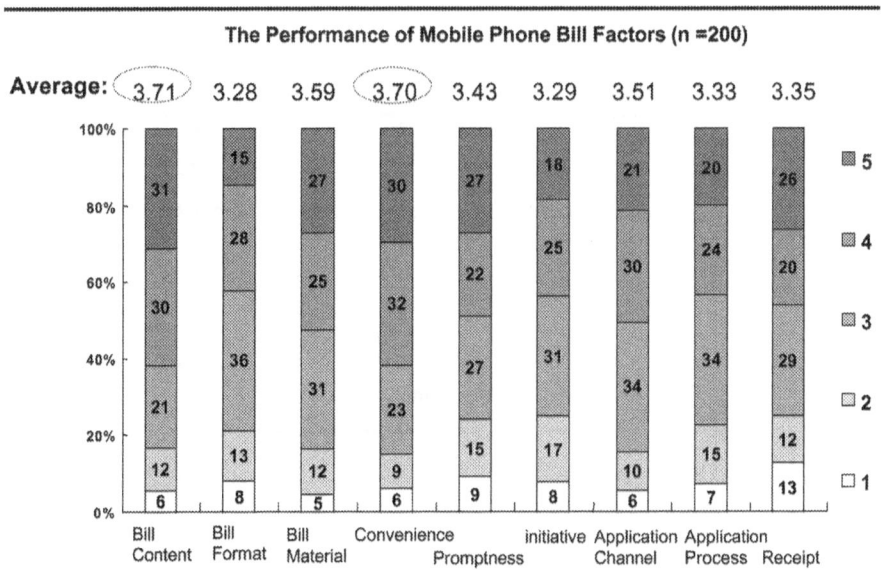

Note: *All figures are rounded.*

Chart 5.4 Customer Satisfaction: Improvement Matrix

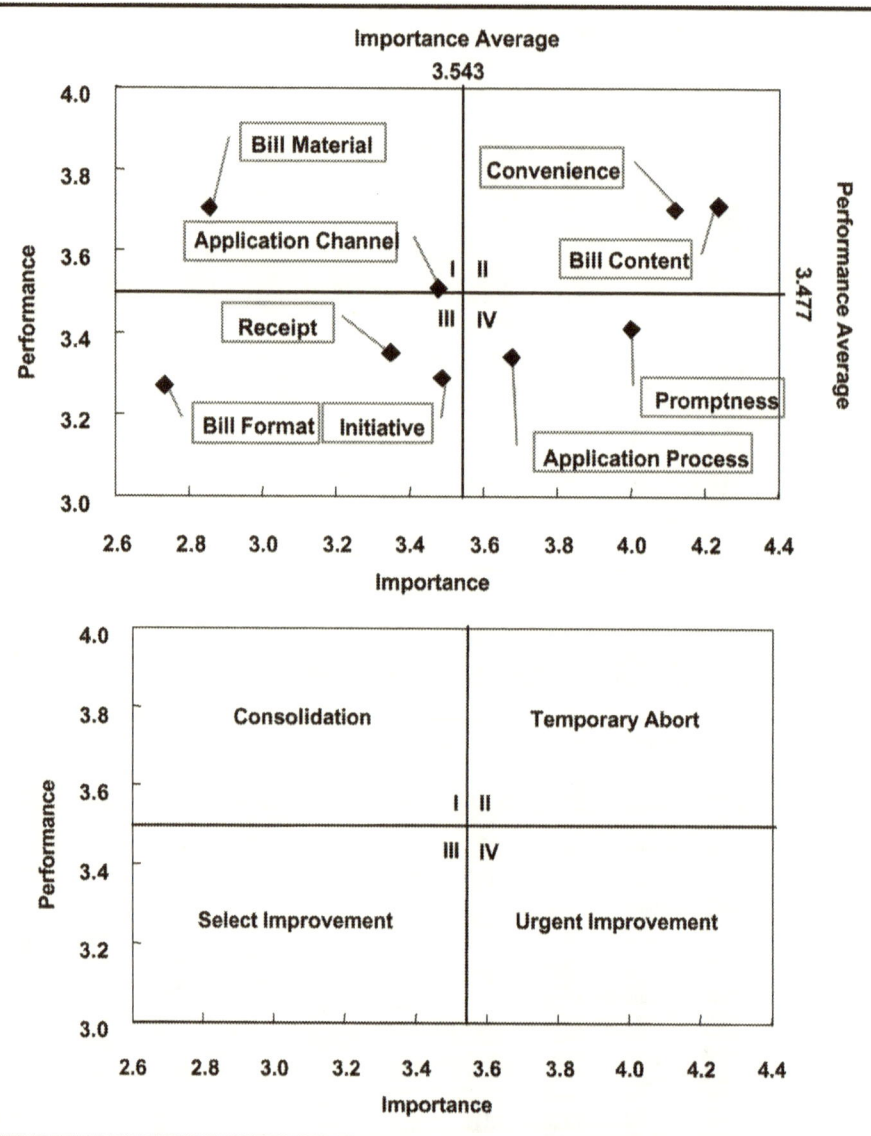

Note: All figures are rounded.

Chart 5.5 Customer Satisfaction: Satisfactor

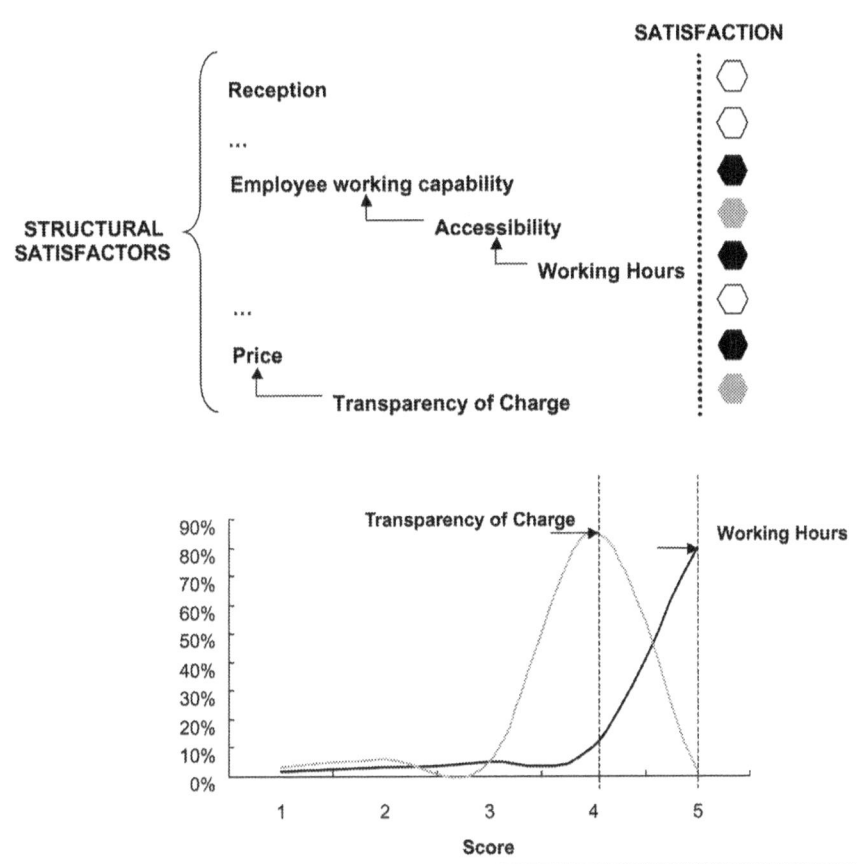

Note: *All figures are rounded.*

From Chart 5.5, in overall satisfacors, price is the weak point which seems the company needs to reduce price to retain customers, employee working capability is another weak point which seems the company needs to take more training for the employees.

Then further step has to be taken to find the causality behind the weak points. From analysis, to improve the transparency of charge seems the best way to make up the weak point of price, not reducing price. Likewise, to expand working hours is the right way for pitfall of employee working capability, not training.

up the weak point of price, not reducing price. Likewise, to expand working hours is the right way for pitfall of employee working capability, not training.

Final step is to question the real contribution of these two ways to the overall satisfaction. Research reflects to expand working hours can contribute more to the satisfaction than to improve the transparency of charge.

Customer Royalty

It is well known that it costs less to keep a customer the company already has than to acquire a new one and that keeping loyalty involves many factors: personal relationships, product quality, customer service, price, and other brand values.

All this makes customer loyalty complicated and hard to quantify. So many business people measure customer satisfaction using surveys and make the mistake of thinking good satisfaction scores mean customer loyalty.

In fact, customer satisfaction scores have little or no correlation with future purchase behavior. Customer satisfaction is transaction-based and product-focused. It measures something that has happened in the past. Loyalty, however, is relationship-based, focused on the overall customer experience and is predictive of how a customer will behave in the future. It's easy to measure a transaction. Measuring a relationship has been difficult if not impossible. Yet the most reliable predictor of how your customer will behave is the strength of that relationship and the secret to measuring it lies in customers' past behavior.

The loyalty index can be classified into 2 categories: controllable factors and external factors illustrated in Chart 5.6. Controllable factors include relationship, experience, offer, brand, price; external factors include personal/situational and market/competition.

Chart 5.6 Customer Loyalty: Loyalty Index

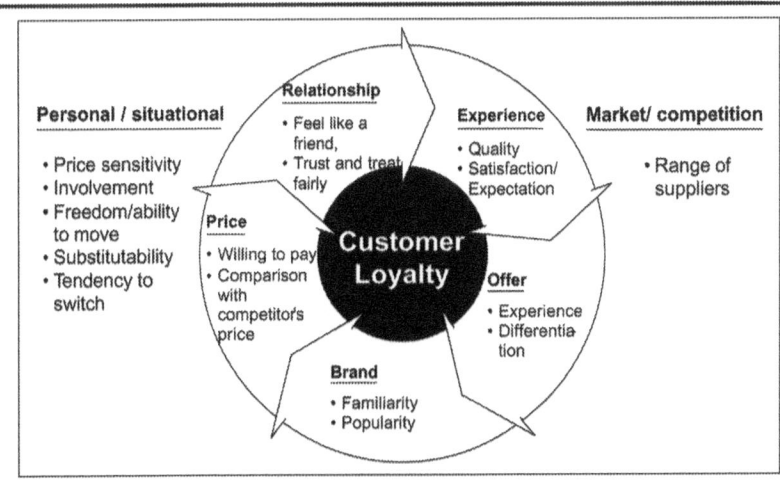

Brand Image

A brand is unlikely to have one brand image, but several, though one or two may predominate. The key in brand image research is to identify or develop the most powerful images and reinforce them through subsequent brand communications. The term "brand image" gained popularity as evidence began to grow that the feelings and images associated with a brand were powerful purchase influencers, though brand recognition, recall and brand identity. It is based on the proposition that consumers buy not only a product (commodity), but also the image associations of the product, such as power, wealth, sophistication, and most importantly identification and association with other users of the brand. In a consumer led world, people tend to define themselves and their Jungian "persona" by their possessions. According to Sigmund Freud, the ego and superego control to a large extent the image and personality that people would like others to have of them.

Good brand images are instantly evoked, are positive, and are almost always unique among competitive brands.

Brand image can be reinforced by brand communications such as packaging, advertising, promotion, customer service, word-of-mouth and other aspects of the brand experience. Brand images are usually evoked by asking consumers the first words/images that come to their mind when a certain brand is mentioned (sometimes called "top of mind"). When responses are highly variable, non-forthcoming, or refer to non-image attributes such as cost, it is an indicator of a weak brand image.

One example of brand image test is shown in Chart 5.7 which illustrated the percentage of overall or a little matching brand image factors.

Chart 5.7 Brand Image: Snaky curve

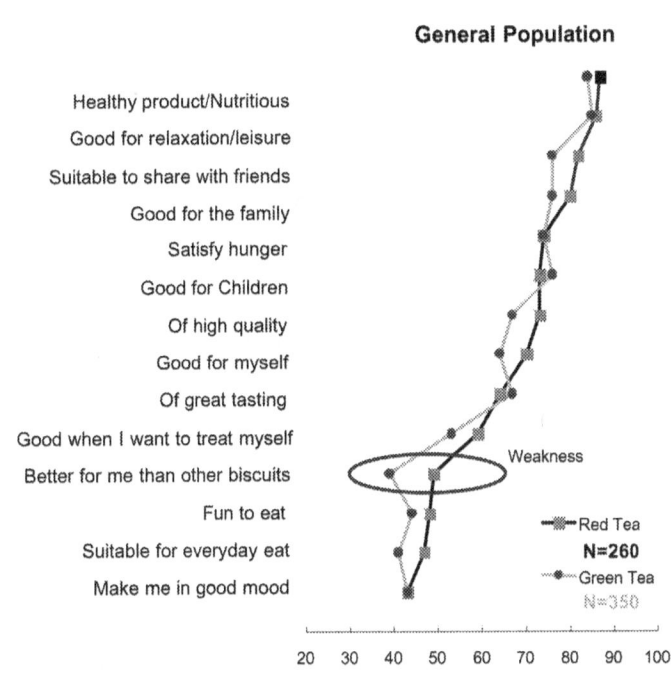

General Population

Healthy product/Nutritious
Good for relaxation/leisure
Suitable to share with friends
Good for the family
Satisfy hunger
Good for Children
Of high quality
Good for myself
Of great tasting
Good when I want to treat myself
Better for me than other biscuits
Fun to eat
Suitable for everyday eat
Make me in good mood

Weakness

Red Tea
N=260
Green Tea
N=350

20 30 40 50 60 70 80 90 100

Note: All figures are rounded.

The brand image can also be perceived from perceptual map shown in Chart 5.8. Two groups of respondents are asked by 2 sets of questions respectively. The first set is which brand to choose for recent purchase, the second set is choose the attributes the brand strongly agree or somewhat agree to. Then calculate the percentage of each attributes of both groups and plot in the map. The averages can be calculated from the percentage of chosen brands.

The image of each brand can be clearly reflected by the vertical distance between the attribute point and brand line which is the line connecting brand point and average cross-point. For example, the brand Siemens has short distance to image point superfluous.

Chart 5.8 Brand Image: Perceptual Map

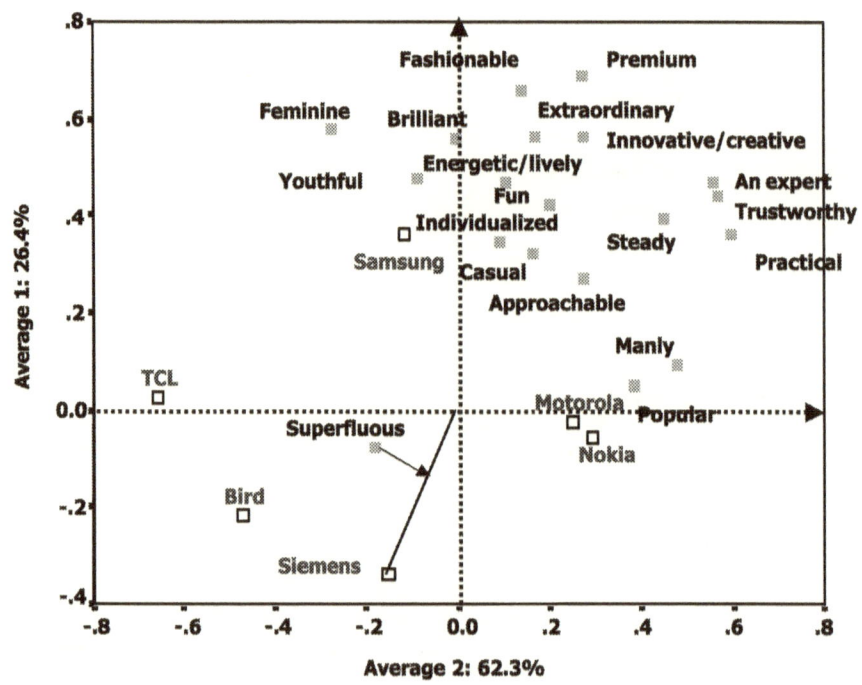

Note: *All figures are rounded.*

Brand Equity

There are many different definitions of brand equity, but they do have several factors in common:

Monetary Value. The amount of additional income expected from a branded product over and above what might be expected from an identical, but unbranded product. For example, grocery stores frequently sell unbranded versions of name brand products. The branded and unbranded products are produced by the same companies, but they carry a generic brand or store brand label like Kroger's or Albertson's. Store brands sell for significantly less than their name brand counterparts, even when the contents are identical. This price differential is the monetary value of the brand name.

Intangible. The intangible value associated with a product that can not be accounted for by price or features. Nike has created many intangible benefits for their athletic products by associating them with star athletes. Children and adults want to wear Nike's products to feel some association with these star athletes ("be like Mike"—for Michael Jordan). It is not the physical features that drive demand for their products, but the marketing image that has been created. Buyers are willing to pay extremely high price premiums over lesser known brands which may offer the same, or better, product quality and features.

Perceived Quality. The overall perceptions of quality and image attributed to a product, independent of its physical features. Mercedes and BMW have established their brand names as synonymous with high-quality, luxurious automobiles. Years of marketing, image building, brand nurturing and quality manufacturing has lead consumers to assume a high level of quality in everything they produce. Consumers are likely to perceive Mercedes and BMW as providing superior quality to other brand name automobiles, even when such a perception is unwarranted.

The overall description of brand equity incorporates the ability to provide added value to your company's products and services. This added value can be used to your company's advantage to charge price premiums, lower marketing costs and offer greater opportunities for customer purchase. A badly mismanaged brand can actually have negative brand equity, meaning that potential customers have such low perceptions of the brand that they prescribe less value to the product than they would if they objectively assessed all its attributes/features.

One of the best examples of brand equity is in the soft drink industry. Without a brand name and all of the marketing dollars that have gone into it, Coca-Cola would be nothing more than flavored water. Due to the company's long-term marketing efforts and protection, enhancement and nurturing of their brand name, Coke is one of the most recognizable brands in the world. However, even this marketing giant has trouble capitalizing on its own brand equity when handled improperly (e.g. New Coke). If someone suddenly took their brand name and brand equity away from them, Coke would lose hundreds of millions, if not billions, of dollars. This includes lost sales, lost marketing dollars and lost promotions, additional marketing costs to promote a new brand, and significantly lower awareness and trial rates for their new brand [3].

Measurement Method

Most evaluations of brand equity involve utility estimation. Specifically, we attempt to measure the value (utility) of a product's features and price level and also measure the overall utility of a product when including brand name. The difference between total utility and the utility of the product features is the value of the brand. In other situations, the utility of the brand is measured directly and added to the feature utilities to produce an overall utility for the product.

Besides utilities, contributing factors such as current awareness levels of each brand, overall perceptions of each brand, and brands currently used should be measured. It is also useful to obtain estimates of marketing, advertising and promotional expenses for the major brands in the market. Together with utility estimates, this information provides a more complete picture of the relative value of each brand and allows you to understand the major forces driving brand equity: product features, price, market awareness, market perceptions and expenditures to build and support those brands. [4]

Brand vs Price

A Brand vs. Price is the simplest method for assessing the relative impact of the brand. Several brands are shown at once and the customer chooses the preferred option. Prices are adjusted and the customer chooses again.

Brand vs. Price is of most use in consumer type markets where there is little to choose functionally between the products—essentially the products are substitutes for one another. For services, industrial and technical type products there can be feature distinctions between the brands and more sophisticated techniques are needed.

Brand vs. functional value

In markets with more complex products where differences in value can be accounted for both by functional differences and the impact of the brand, getting at the value of the brand alone is more complex than for simple products and relies on a multi-stage approach. In the first stage it is necessary to identify the value of the functional parts of the product unbranded. What premium does a bigger engine, or better fuel economy command? To understand the value of different products functionally, conjoint analysis is the most powerful and effective tool.

The second stage is to introduce brand to the mix. Knowing how different functional combinations are valued, by introducing brand you can measure changes that the brand makes on selection compared to to the unbranded. By careful calibration, it is possible to uncover the value of the brand over and above the functional differences. For product development and pricing purposes, this allows managers to determine whether resources should be focused on strengthening the brand and perceived value, or on strengthening the underlying product offer.

Brand vs. Financial value

Some companies measure brand equity completely differently, relying on financial measures of brand performance. Because strong brands have extra value to customers, the brands themselves are able to command a higher price in the market, not just to end users, but also through the distribution channel in the form of reduced margins compared to other similar products. An alternative to making a research-based evaluation of brand equity is therefore to look at the premium, or value-add from the brand financially in comparison to equivalent products. This can be carried out either in terms of gross margin, or in wider measures such as EVA (economic value added). [5]

Pricing

Market context and positioning are also extremely important in setting prices. In technology markets, prices are typically falling over time. Historically the price of PCs has been dropping at about 2% per month. In business markets "value-in-use" or "total cost" may be more important than absolute price.

Pricing surveys and value research are always of great interest to managers faced with determining the merits of increasing profit margins by raising prices, or the likelihood of increasing revenues by decreasing prices. Various price test methods are being used in research to achieve marketing expectation. Each of the methods available to measure consumer response to various prices can be applied at the product concept stage and for existing products.

The most common approach to pricing research is to rely on market intelligence and follow-my-leader type pricing using a competitor as a benchmark. However a me-too approach leads to high levels of competition, and it is important to consider the strategic impact of pricing as well as the short term sales impact.

Some caution is needed when conducting pricing studies. Statistically speaking, where you are looking to optimise prices where you are looking at relatively small price changes of 5-10%, you will need larger than normal sample sizes to get the statistical accuracy you need. For many companies this can make pricing research expensive, unless combined with a range of other measurement.

■   Rating scales

Rating scales often are used to provide graded scales that indicate importance or acceptability of a given concept. Their application within online pricing surveys usually involves determining (1) the degree of importance that consumers attach to a given price level. This approach reports the overall importance of price and not the optimal price for a given product or brand. Price importance, along with measures of other attribute importance constructs is useful in segmenting respondents into key market segment groups.

Pricing questions or pricing scales can alternatively include such measures as (2) the likelihood of trial, (3) the likelihood of purchase at given price points, or (4) the overall acceptability of a series of price points can be measured. These pricing measures would be repeated for multiple price points, thereby allowing the researcher to pinpoint the optimal price for a given product. Multiple price points or pricing questions must be used.

■ Direct Method

This method calls for asking the respondent direct questions about price effects. The researcher might begin by asking if a respondent is currently buying a certain product. If the answer is yes, the researcher would ask would the respondent continue purchasing the product if the respondent had to pay $5 extra, $10 extra, etc., until the respondent no longer expressed an interest. This method is similar to "dollar metric" approaches used in the 1960's to test how many additional cents would it take to get you to switch from "Coke" to "7up". Respondents were presented with all possible brand combinations and would indicate how much they were willing to pay for one brand over another.

While at first glance, this method bears some similarity to the Van Westendorp method (discussed below), the researcher—and not the consumer—must create the various price-points to include in the questionnaire. Furthermore, perceptual issues that invariably enter decision making are not addressed in this method.

■ Gabor-Granger Method

Gabor-Granger pricing research is named after the economists who invented it in the 1960s. Customers are asked to complete a survey where they are asked to say if they would buy a product at a particular price. The price is changed and respondents again say if they would buy or not. From the results we can work out what the optimum price is for each individual. By taking a sample of customers we can work out what levels of demand would be expected at each price point across the market as a whole (the demand curve). Using this estimate of demand, the price elasticity (or expected revenue) can be calculated and so the optimum price-point in the market established shown in Chart 5.9.

Chart 5.9 Price Test: Gabor-Granger Output

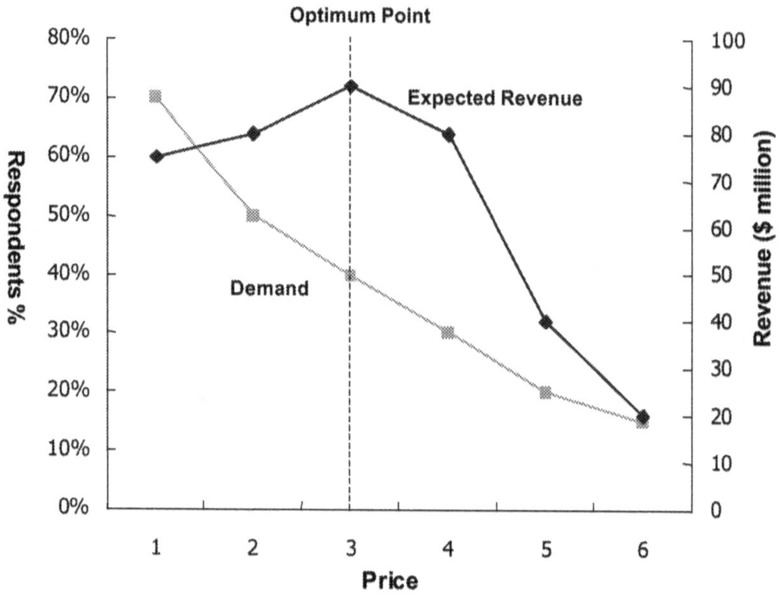

Note: All figures are rounded.

A weakness of Gabor Granger is that customers may understate the price they will pay (there are also circumstances in which they will overstate the price). Consequently the phrasing of the "would you buy" question is extremely important as are other contextual questions to place the customer in the buying frame of mind. Typically, Gabor Granger is only used when considering one product in isolation, whereas in real life they would face a choice about which product to buy.

■ Van Westendorp Method—Price Sensitivity Meter (PSM)

This method includes a series of questions designed to provide price perceptions to four questions based upon product descriptions. The questions ask the respondent to indicate: (1) the price at which the product is so cheap that the respondent would question its quality; (2) the price at which the product is inexpensive, but no so inexpensive that the respondent would question its quality; (3) the price at which the product is expensive, but not so expensive that the respondent would consider it; and (4) the price at which the product is so expensive that the respondent would not consider it.

Analysis of the data yields several distributions shown in the following diagrams (Chart 5.10). Various intersections on the curves yield inputs for pricing decisions.

Chart 5.10 Price Test: Respondents' Perception of Price/Value

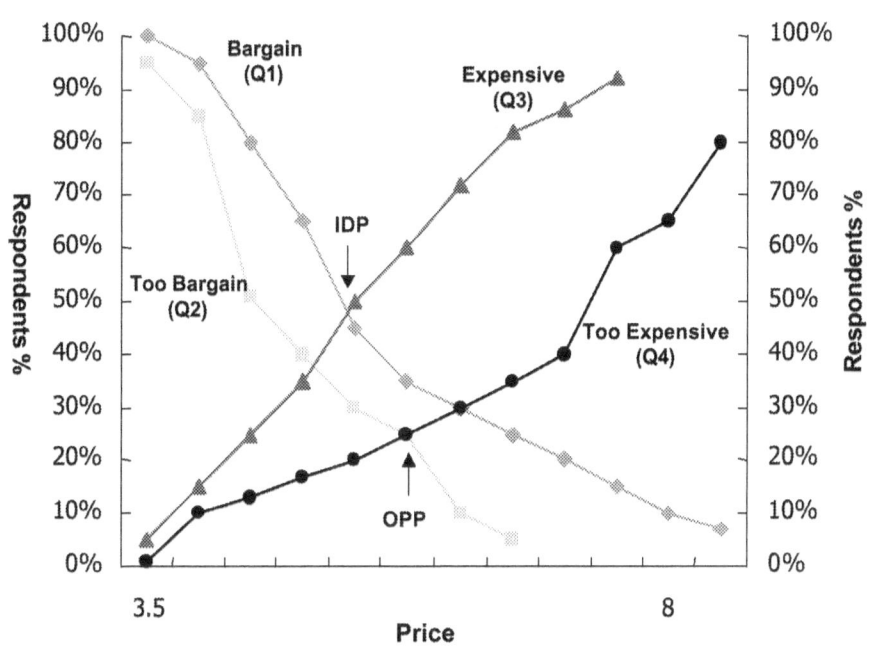

Note: All figures are rounded.

The IDP is the point on the price scale where the number of respondets who regard the price as a bargain is equal to the number of respondents who regard the price as expensive. According to Van Westendorp, this generally represents either the median price actually paid by consumers or the price of the product of an important market leader. IDP is based on costumers' experience with price levels in the market and will change with market conditions.

The OPP is the price at which the number of respondents who see the product as too cheap is equal to the number who see the product as too expensive. This is typically the recommended price in PSM.

In Chart 5.11, the "not expensive" and "not bargain" curves are 1-% accumulations for the "expensive" and "bargain" data.

The range of prices between the Point of Marginal Cheapness (PMC) and the Point of Marginal Expensiveness (PME) is the Range of Acceptable Prices for a product. According to Van Westendorp, in established markets, few competitive products are priced outside this range.

Chart 5.11 Price Test: Range of acceptable price

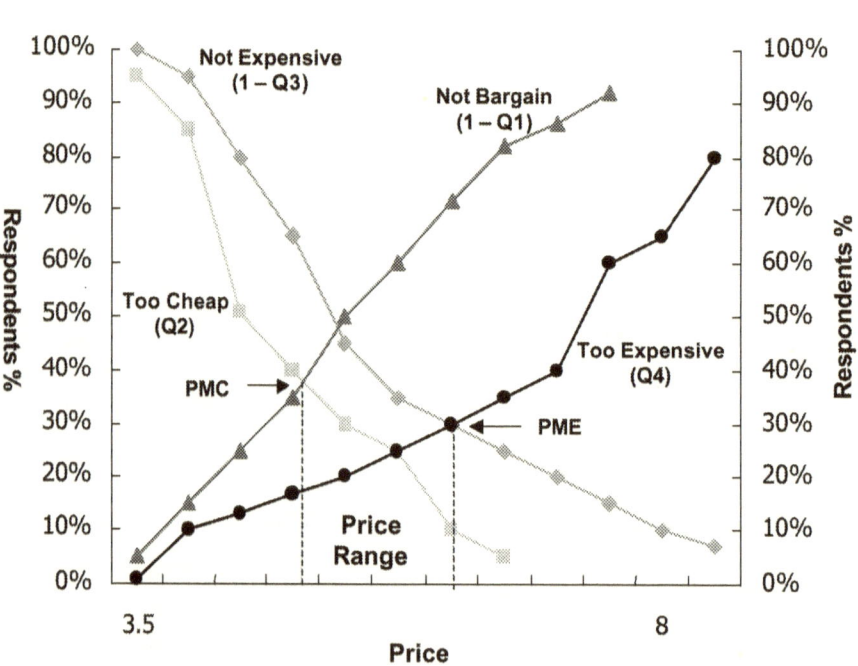

Note: All figures are rounded.

From the cumulative distributions of these price points, certain pricing decisions can be made. For an established product category, prices may represent price expectations. At prices slightly higher than the expected prices, purchase intent drops sharply. However, at slightly lower prices, purchase intent does not increase dramatically. (In more technical terms, expected demand would be relatively elastic just above the expected price, and relatively inelastic just below the expected price.)

Normally, the outcome of a Van Westendorp study demonstrates that, regardless of the product description, users of a product are much more likely than non-users to purchase at every feasible price. (In other words, the expected demand curve for users lies well above the demand curve for non-users.)

Weaknesses of the Van Westendorp technique include the inability to equate price perceptions and propensity to buy. Note that often people prefer an expensive product over a cheaper alternative, but this may not be the case in when it comes time to make a purchase. In addition, the "optimal" pricing point recommended by this analysis is based solely on consumer

■ Experimental Test Market

This method involves comparing price changes and their effects in a real world situations. For example, if prices vary vastly by channel of distribution (i.e., grocery store, discount, and specialty store), the demand for the product in each of these channels can be compared. This method's main advantage is that real world behavior is observed and quantified. However, this assumes other marketing factors will remain constant while the effects of price changes are measured. Moreover, the method is costly, can be time consuming, and only measures "self elasticity" (i.e., demand for one's own brand) and not "cross-elasticity" (demand for competitor's brand) with any precision.

■ Econometric models

Tracking the effects of pricing on market share over an extended period of time gives a unique view of price demand relationships. Monthly or quarterly measures show changes that result from marketing programs, competitive action, or general market demand. These trend analysis studies estimate price-demand relationships, and can show the interaction between price and brand sales if market measures of price changes are included. However, this method says little about the interaction between brand and price, and simply focuses on price variations of various products and their relationship to demand. The Van Westendorp method, conjoint analysis, and discrete choice models, are by contrast, pliable enough measure the effects of brand on price.

■   Full Profile Conjoint Analysis

In full profile conjoint analysis, a sample of respondents are asked to rate or rank a set of product profiles. For example, a product profile might be composed of four attributes. Take an express mail service. Such a service is composed of many attributes like brand, delivery time, price/document, and drop-off location to name a few. For each attribute, the levels of the attributes are varied. For example, with an express mail service, the "levels" of brand might include FedEx, UPS, Airborne, or the Post Office.

The conjoint analysis profiles present different combinations representing express mail services. To these profiles respondents state their preference. The design of conjoint analysis combinations is non-trivial and must be done using experimental design methodology. The conjoint analysis process a set of utility functions for each respondent measured, for segments within the sample, and for the total sample. Utility functions show the demand curve or relative importance of each attribute and each level of each attribute.

Conjoint permits a thorough understanding of the relative leverage of each attribute and each level within the attribute, primarily by using a simulation that permits an analysis of the sensitivity of changes in the levels of these attributes on the total sample's share of preference. It also permits the researcher to determine the effects on consumers from changes in attribute levels. However, the model assumes that consumer utilities are linear and additive, and this may not be the case in the real world.

Chart 5.12 Price Test: Full Profile Conjoint Analysis Sample—Car

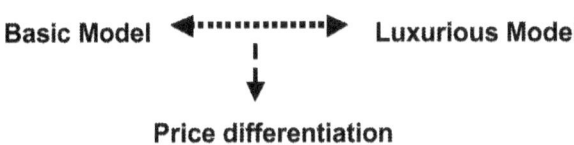

Basic Model ◀••••••••••••▶ **Luxurious Model**

Price differentiation

Model	Engine	Drive train	Brake	Airbags	Fr Seat	Material	Climate	Color	Price ($)
Bas 1	2.3L	LFD	None	Neither	Non-adjusted	Fabric	Mech	Silver	1.7-2.0K
Bas 2	...	...	...	...	...	...	...	...	2.0-2.2K
Bas 3	...	...	...	...	...	...	...	...	2.2-2.5K
Bas 4	...	...	...	...	...	...	...	...	2.5-2.7K
Lux 1	2.3L	L3V	Both	Both	Adjusted (6D)	Leather	Auto	Silver	2.2-2.5K
Lux 2	...	...	...	...	...	...	...	...	2.5-2.7K
Lux 3	...	...	...	...	...	...	...	...	2.7-3.0K
Lux 4	...	...	...	...	...	...	...	...	3.0-3.2K
									3.2-3.5K

Note: All figures are rounded.

■ Self-Explicated Conjoint Analysis

The self-explicated conjoint model provides a simple alternative producing utility score estimates equal to or superior to that of full-profile and other popular approaches such as Adaptive Conjoint Analysis. The self-explicated model is based theoretically on the multi-attribute attitude models that combine attribute importance with attribute desirability to estimate overall preference.

Initially, all attribute levels are presented to respondents for evaluation to eliminate any levels that would not be acceptable in a product under any conditions. Next, attribute levels are presented and each level is evaluated for desirability. Finally, based on these evaluations, the most desirable levels of all attributes are evaluated relative importance. As with the full-profile model, these scores can be summed and simulations run to obtain a score for any profile of interest. This simple self-reporting approach is easier for the respondent to complete and straightforward in terms of determining the importance or desirability of attributes and attribute levels. [6]

■   Brand/Price Trade-off

This choice-based modeling technique specifically studies the interaction between brand and price on consumer choice. The method calls for replacing product factors with brand. Researchers using this method vary prices instead of product profiles. From this, one can glean information about both self-elasticity and cross-elasticity with other brands.

■   Discrete-Choice Model

Discrete-choice modeling is best employed when the focal point of the research is not only to determine consumer acceptance of various prices but also to assess the influence that features have on adding brand value. Briefly, in a discrete choice study, the researcher is interested in observing how choices are made and their outcomes.

When choosing a particular brand of clothing, consumers often associate that brand with a set of attributes, such as its price, style, fit, color, and type of material. Each individual consumer makes his/her choice based on the utility he/she assigns to each attribute. Utility functions can be derived from the choices of consumer segments, and these functions include expressions "that capture effects due to differences in the attribute values of competing alternatives and/or differences in the characteristics" of the consumer under study.

As in the brand/price trade-off approach, respondents do not merely indicate their preference for a given brand, but rather indicate a choice for a particular product.

A discrete choice offers some advantages over a ratings based approach like conjoint analysis. Unlike conjoint, discrete choice asks respondents to choose from a group of products and offers them the alternative of choosing none of the products under evaluation. Discrete choicer permits the researcher to estimate unique demand curves for all brands in the study and incorporate these interactions in a simulation model of the market. This permits a thorough review of interactions, especially the role brand plays in price. Discrete choice also places products choices into a competitive context. Most importantly, unlike conjoint analysis, discrete choice market simulations assume an S-shaped response curve; discrete choice utilities are estimates of the probability of choosing a given product. Thus the resulting values come as close as possible to the actual percentages of respondents choosing each product concept.

Advertising

Five questions are critical in marketing communications and the creation of advertising. These are Who (Spokesperson), Says What (Advertising Message), To Whom (Target Audience), How (Which Media Channel), With What Effect (Desired Outcome).

Brand Connection [7]

When any advertising research is conducted we must have in mind the Advertising Effect or desired outcome. If we can determine the effect, the other answers to the other four questions can be answered.

Brand connect products or services to people. This connection is through the meaning that the brand brings into the lives the people that use it. Brands tap into six mode of communication to convey meaning. These modes are instrumental in determining advertising effect:

- Naming
- Wording
- Describing
- Picturing
- Symbolizing
- Animating

The personal benefits and values of the core product are reinforced and strengthened as the brand meaning grows and it becomes more connected to the person. In the language of a brand manager, the result is a high equity brand that is surrounded by loyal customers.

The energy drink "Red Bull" pays college students to drive around campus with a huge display can of Red Bull strapped to the roof of their car. Many college students watch TV infrequently and TV ads are only used to remind the targeted younger audience of product benefits.

Measuring the effectiveness of an advertising using means-ends analysis and hierarchical values maps requires a series of measurement components. The following are a sampling of items from different advertising evaluations using the Means-ends methodology:

Communicated Messages

What attributes or features does this ad communicate?

- Taste: This drink has great taste
- Energy: This drink provides an energy boost
- Reliability: This computer is reliable and trouble free
- Features: This computer has the features I'm looking for in a laptop
- Cost: This computer is less expensive than most major brands
- Style: This coat is attractive and stylish

Communicated Benefits

What benefits does this ad communicate?

- Comfort: This car is comfortable to ride in
- Value: This car is a good value for the money
- Origin: This car is superior to most imports
- Quality: This car is a quality vehicle

Personal Values

What personal values does this ad communicate? This ad reminds me...

- Need Fulfillment: This car will meet my driving needs
- Caring: This company cares about my needs
- Trust: I can trust the car I drive
- Understanding: The company understands the needs of this car's buyers

Higher Order Values

Higher order values are the over arching values that drive our behavior and give meaning to life. Products and services are more likely to be purchased if they are consistent with these values. Measures of these values should be included in advertising studies.

This ad brings to mind...

- Accomplishment: The good feelings of personal accomplishment
- Pease of Mind: The good feeling of having peace of mind
- Personal Satisfaction: The good feeling about myself and what I do
- Security: The good feeling of personal security and well being

Ad Effectiveness

Behavioral and attitudinal goals will vary by ad and include such factors as:

- Realism: This ad shows a realistic view of President Bush
- Entertainment Value: This ad is entertaining to watch
- Relevance: This ad provides relevant information about the products
- Ad Reinforcement: This ad reinforces positive feelings about this product
- Information: This ad makes me want to learn more about this product
- Purchase: This ad makes me more likely to purchase this product
- Attention: This ad really holds my attention

Advertising Tests

Several advertising test methods have been developed to measure the advertising effect and brand connection such as storyboard quality test, Ad test before release, TV ad test, etc.

- Storyboard test

  The main purchase of this test is to measure which story is more acceptable to public. It can be categorized into 2 types:
  - Monadic Test
  - Comparative Test

  Monadic Test includes "Gut-level" impression, comprehension (content recall, key message), easy-to-understand, believability, relevance, uniqueness, diagnostic, product perception, user imagery, persuasion (purchase intent & why).

- Before exposure test

  The main purpose of this test is to measure the possible advertising effect of the ad. It includes persuasion (post-exposure ~ pre-exposure/comparison/recommendation), recall (ad awareness (product/brand)/content), diagnosis (key message/likes & dislikes/attractiveness & believability & easy-to-understand), brand imagery, purchase intent.

- TV Express

  The main purpose of the TV test is to measure the persuasion of the TV ad, shown in Chart 5.13 The certain sample based respondents are recruited to the test center. They are required to watch two types of ad sample video tapes. The first is made of various advertising excluding test ad, the second is made of various advertising including test ad. The respondents are required to choose brands after twice watch. The researchers will keep eyes on the difference. Then one day later, the respondents are asked to tell what they remember about that advertising to test the brand recall. Then, the respondents are divided into 2 groups of test sample and blank sample. The test sample are required to watch the test ad again. Both 2 groups will be asked the questions of purchase preference, brand image and brand equity.

Chart 5.13 Advertising: TV Express

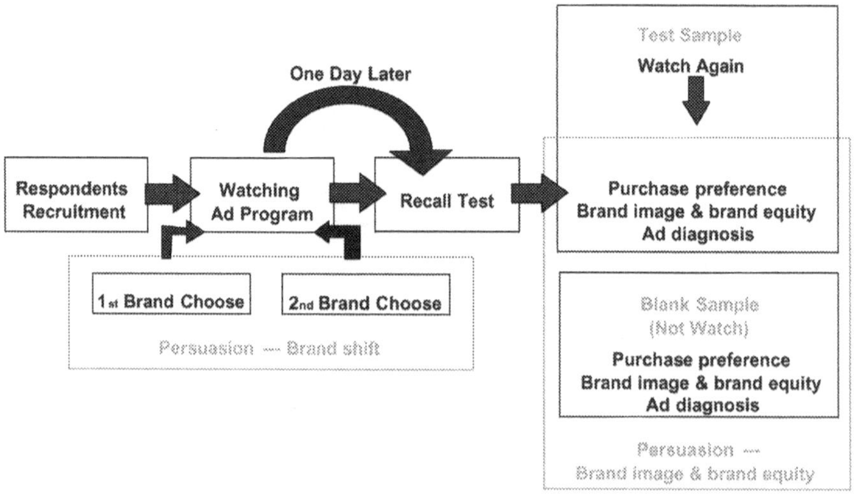

■ Print Express

The main purpose of the print express test is to measure the persuasion of the print ad. The key steps of the test process are illustrated in Chart 5.14 which is similar to TV express. The certain sample based respondents are recruited to the test center. Two groups of respondents are required to read 2 ad sample pamphlet respectively. One pamphlet is made of various advertising including test picture with brand, the other is made of various advertising including test picture without brand. One day later, two groups of respondents are asked to tell what they remember about that advertising to test the brand recall. Some respondents are required to recall with reminders. Then, the respondents are divided into 2 groups of test sample and blank sample. The test sample are required to watch the test ad again. Both 2 groups will be asked the questions of purchase preference, brand image and brand equity.

Chart 5.14 Advertising: Print Express

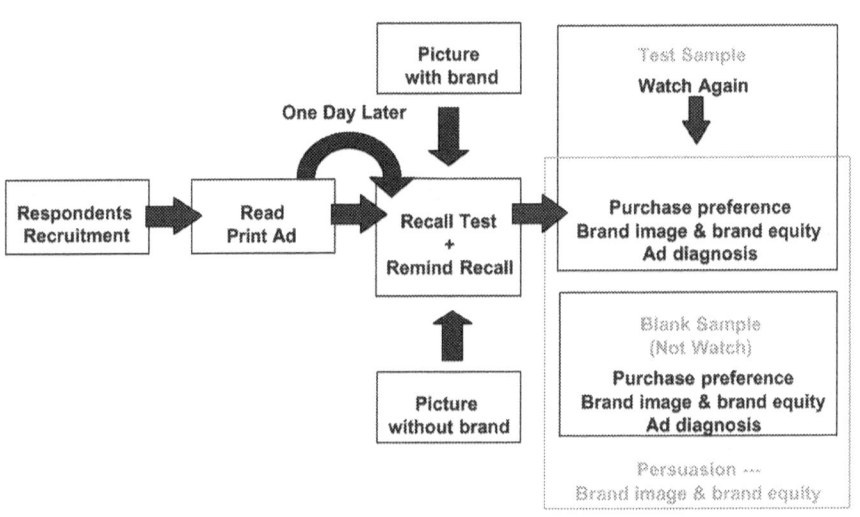

Notes and References

[1] Market Segmentations Survey, **www.surveyz.com** Copyright 2000-2005

[2] Smith and Albaum, Fundamentals of Marketing Research, Sage Publications, 2005

[3] What Is Brand Equity?, Understanding Brand Equity, White Papers Library: Strategy Research, www.dssresearch.com

[4] How Do You Measure Brand Equity?, Understanding Brand Equity, White Papers Library: Strategy Research, www.dssresearch.com

[5] Brand equity and brand value, www.dobney.com

[6] Srinivasan, V., Surprising robustness of the self-explicated approach to customer preference structure measurement. Journal of Marketing Research, 34, 286-291. (1997, May).

[7] Online Advertising surveys and research, www.surveyz.com

978-0-595-36401-5
0-595-36401-2